MW01442398

THE SOCIAL WORK OF THE SALVATION ARMY

by Edwin Gifford Lamb

Originally published in 1909.

PREFACE.

I use the word "Social" in the title of this work to suggest that, save in an auxiliary way, I am not attempting to describe the religious features of the organization. Such a field of investigation would prove a very profitable and interesting one, but it is a field, which, for the sake of clearness and impartial study, should be kept separate. The organization itself recognizes the primary division. Commander Booth-Tucker, the leader of the Army in the United States from 1896 to 1904, says, "The Salvation Army is the evolution of two great ideas: first, that of reaching with the gospel of salvation the masses who are outside the pale of ordinary church influence, and second, that of caring for their temporal as well as spiritual interests." [1]

I have secured very little data from books, as there is but little authentic literature on the subject. Primarily, the data for this treatise were taken from personal observation. In pursuing the subject I have visited Salvation Army social institutions of every description. In addition to visiting the larger cities of the United States and the three Army colonies, situated in Ohio, Colorado and California, respectively, I have investigated the work in London, where the Army had its origin, and at the farm colony in Hadleigh, on the river Thames, some thirty miles from London. I have slept in the hotels, worked in the industrial homes, wandered over the farm colonies, and mingled with the inmates of other types of Army institutions.

Nov., 1909. E. G. L.

[1] Pamphlet "The Salvation Army in the United States."

TABLE OF CONTENTS.

Preface

Introduction

CHAPTER I The Salvation Army Industrial Department

CHAPTER II The Salvation Army Hotels and Lodging Houses

CHAPTER III The Farm Colonies of the Salvation Army

CHAPTER IV The Salvation Army Slum Department

CHAPTER V The Salvation Army Rescue Department

CHAPTER VI Some Minor Features of the Salvation Army Social Work

CHAPTER VII Conclusion

CHAPTER I.

Introduction.

The Salvation Army was founded by William Booth in London, England, in 1865. Previous to this time Mr. Booth had been a successful clergyman in the Methodist Church, and had become widely known throughout England as a revivalist. As time passed, he had become more and more interested in the condition of the un-churched masses, and as his church did not approve of his taking up work among the masses in connection with it as an organization, he had, in 1861, separated from the Methodists. With little support, he established in London what was known as The Christian Mission.

From the first, numbers of converts were made, and soon several missions were established in London, and other cities of England. From the first, too, the agency of women was an important feature. Especially was this true in visitation among the lower classes. In regard to the foundation of the Army itself and in connection with its earlier successes, much credit must be given to Mrs. Booth, the wife of William Booth. She became as noted a speaker and revivalist as her husband, and together, they made plans for the movement. Unfortunately she died of cancer in 1890. Through these early years of the movement its management, almost unconsciously, developed along lines that were military in form. At first the title of "Captain" was used among the sailors and fishermen to designate the local leader of the company, and then it was extended wherever, among the rough element, the "Mr." or "Rev." would seem out of place. The usage and the spirit accompanying it soon spread, and by the year 1879 military methods and titles were officially added. The Rev. Wm. Booth, who, up to this time, had been known as "Superintendent of the Christian Mission," became "General" Booth, and the "Mission" became the "Salvation Army." [2]

This addition of military methods seems to have accelerated the movement by favoring efficient and systematic control. Soon after this time, we find, the organization had spread to the United States, Canada, Australia, France, Switzerland, Holland, Belgium, Scandinavia, Germany and Italy. Then missionary work was taken up in India, and later on, in Africa, Java and Japan. At the present time (1908), according to its reports, the Army occupies fifty-two different countries and colonies. In no country has its rate of progress been more remarkable than in the United States, where in point of numbers, the local organization now ranks second only to that of Great Britain. [3]

Along with the rapid growth went a differentiation almost as rapid and unique as the growth itself. In fact, both reacted on each other. The work was separated first into three main departments, viz.: Spiritual, Social and Trade. It will be necessary to make a brief statement of this differentiation in detail. In the Spiritual Department we have the extension of the original idea, that of converting the people. Corps, as the different religious groups were called, sprang up and multiplied until even the smaller towns were occupied. Converts were added by hundreds and thousands. Large numbers of the brightest and best of these converts were utilized in extending the work still further, and after undergoing a brief training, were sent out, some to aid the movement in the mother country, others to begin the work in different parts of Europe and in America, and still others as missionaries to all parts of the world. Meanwhile, the work in each local organization or Corps, became systematized, and the Corps were united into Sections or Divisions, the Divisions into larger districts called Provinces, and the Provinces into Commands, which for the most part controlled the territory of an entire country. Each of these divisions from the Corps to the Command, was delegated to an officer who had sole charge, and who was responsible to the officer above him. For example, the United States, at present, is divided into two Commands; the first extending from New York to Chicago; the second from Chicago to the Pacific Coast. The first Command has six Provinces; the second, four. Each Province has from three to nine Divisions, and each Division contains a number of Corps. Thus, while each Corps is complete in itself, the general administration is very highly centralized; so much so, that an order from General Booth at the National Headquarters, London, England, must be obeyed by every Corps in the world.

While the organization of the Spiritual Department was taking place in this manner, the Social Work was assuming large proportions, and differentiating itself. Visitation in the lower parts of the cities was organized into a regular department of Slum Work, called the Slum Department, with a specialized corps of officers. Work among fallen women was instituted as the Rescue Department, with its rescue homes and trained workers. The establishment of hotels and lunch counters for both men and women became finally what is now the Social Department. The wood yards and small factories, together with the salvage depots and cheap stores, were organized into the Industrial Department. Work among the children resulted in the establishment of kindergartens and orphanages. The colonization enterprise took root, and was divided into the industrial colonies and farm colonies. Thus, we have here a differentiation of the original Social Department into six distinct divisions, which we shall consider separately in this treatise. As these lines of work advanced, although each had its special group of workers, it was natural that the work should follow the administrative system of Commands, Provinces, Divisions and Corps, which had already been marked out in the Spiritual Department.

The third primary division, that of trade, has had some interesting developments. There is, for example, the trade carried on in articles necessary to the members of the Army themselves, and which they cannot conveniently obtain in the open market, such as uniforms, badges, books and musical instruments. The Reliance Trading Company, for instance, was incorporated in 1902, under the laws of the State of New Jersey. This company owns and publishes the "War Cry," the official gazette of the Army in the United States; does the printing for the various departments of the Army; manufactures fountain pens; makes uniforms, bonnets and hats for the Army members; conducts an Insurance Department, and carries on other business enterprises. [4]

There is, too, the trade in the products of the various factories and industries connected with the relief work of the Army. For example, the Salvation Army Industrial Homes Company, incorporated in New Jersey, has greatly facilitated the industrial work in the United States. There have been companies formed and organized as building societies, insurance companies, and a Salvation Army Bank.

In all these companies the Salvation Army, through its officers, always has control, although it invites and seeks investments from the public. The following extract, taken from a prospectus sent out by the Salvation Army Industrial Homes Company, illustrates the point:

"The Charter of our Industrial Homes Co. has been prepared by Messrs. Jas. B. Dill & Co., the eminent corporation lawyers, who have kindly given us the full benefit of their skill and experience, at a fairly nominal charge. The capital consists of $500,000.00, divided into 50,000 shares, of the par value of $10.00 each, of which 25,000 are in 6% cumulative preferred stock and 25,000 in common stock. Only the preferred shares are offered to the public, and bear interest at 6%, which is guaranteed by the Army. The common shares are held by the Army, with a view to retaining the control of the company, and the entire profits, over and above the interest on the preferred stock, are thus devoted to the charitable and religious work of the Army, and help us to continually expand and enlarge our homes." ... "We shall be happy to supply any information or answer any questions as to the financial standing of the Salvation Army. For our spiritual and social operations in the United States, we have now an annual income of nearly $2,000,000.00, while the value of our real estate holdings in this country amount to about $1,500,000. Hence, it will be seen that in guaranteeing the interest upon these preferred shares, amounting in all to only $15,000.00, we are abundantly able to insure the regular payment of the same apart, altogether, from the income of our industrial homes."

As a result of this rapid growth along the three lines described, the movement everywhere forced itself upon public recognition. The publication of its weekly organ, the "War Cry," in many different languages and countries aided its growth. Other magazines of higher class and better quality were issued. At the same time, the public press investigated the organization, and for a long time criticised it harshly. In fact, during all this time, while so successful, the Army suffered much persecution. The crowds of people composed of those whom it was seeking to benefit, seemed often to be its worst enemies, and then, to make matters more difficult, the police, we are told, instead of furnishing protection, often, themselves, joined in the persecution. There were many instances, in this early period, where the enthusiastic reformers were ill treated and even fatally injured. There was, however, some reason for all this persecution. A movement so sudden and apparently so contrary to existing institutions, needed time for its real principle to become known. The external manifestation seemed to consist of nothing but defiant disregard of established religious custom and ceremonial. Thus, while the vital principle of love for humanity was working its way into individual lives and attracting them to the ranks of the organization, the world at large openly showed its antagonism. Gradually, however, the sense of public opposition and antagonism grew less. Gradually the knowledge that, behind the superficial emotionalism, were depths of disinterested sympathy for fellow men and women worked itself into the public mind. Attacks on Army groups on street corners became less frequent, and when they did occur, were suppressed by the police. The press ceased its bitter criticism.

It was about this time that renewed and increased attention was focused on the new movement by the publication in

1890 of General Booth's famous book, "In Darkest England, and the Way Out." In some ways the book served to mark a new epoch in the development of that part of practical sociology which concerns itself with the direct betterment of the lower class of society. The old method of dealing with the poor is ably described by Ruskin, when he says:

"We make our relief either so insulting to them, or so painful that they rather die than take it at our hands; or, for third alternative, we leave them so untaught and foolish, that they starve like brute creatures, wild and dumb, not knowing what to do, or what to ask." [5]

This was a point of view which in its relation to the degraded elements of society was an expression of sympathy rather than of harsh criticism and mistrust. Although it had been set forth by others previously, it had never before forced itself so strongly on the public. In addition, the daring statements and bold theories, given utterance in "Darkest England," served to surprise all schools of reform. The public consciousness had never before faced the problem in such a way. It was aroused, and began to ask questions. The book ran through edition after edition. It was printed in a cheap form and within a short time was circulated all over the civilized world.

In his "scheme" General Booth laid down seven fundamental principles, which he claimed were essential to success. They were as follows:

1. The first principle that must be bore in mind, as governing every scheme that may be put forward, is that it must change the man, when it is his character and conduct

which constitute the reasons for his failure in the battle of life.

2. The remedy, to be effectual, must change the circumstances of the individual, when they are the cause of his wretched condition, and lie beyond his control.

3. Any remedy worthy of consideration must be on a scale commensurate with the evil with which it proposes to deal.

4. Not only must the scheme be large enough, but it must be permanent.

5. But while it must be permanent, it must be made practicable.

6. The indirect features of the scheme must not be such as to produce injury to the persons whom we seek to benefit.

7. While assisting one class of the community, it must not seriously interfere with the interests of another. [6]

General Booth's personal attitude, also, is well worth noting. In the preface of his book he makes the following statement:

"I do not claim that my scheme is either perfect in its details, or complete in the sense of being adequate to combat all forms of gigantic evils, against which it is, in the main, directed. Like other human things, it must be perfected through suffering; but it is a sincere endeavor to do something, and to do it on principles, which can be instantly applied and universally developed." [7]

And again, in view of some of the manifestations of the organization as we see it, the following is interesting, as coming from its founder. He says: "But one of the grimmest social problems of our time should be sternly faced, not with a view to the generation of profitless emotions, but with a view to its solution." [8]

Upon the publication of this book there arose a division of opinion in regard to the scheme which was set forth. On the one hand, numbers of noted philanthropists aided General Booth with money and moral support. On the other hand, there was opposition from a certain class of reformers, headed by that eminent scientist, Thomas Huxley. This opposition, however, did not so much attack the principles advocated, as the agency for their application, namely, the Salvation Army, itself, characterized in Huxley's words as "Autocratic socialism, masked by its theological exterior." [9]

From that time to the present many thoughtful men have continued this opposition to the Army as an agent of social service. Further on we shall consider the validity and strength of their arguments. At that time the press on all sides took up the controversy, and it was finally decided to appoint a committee of investigation to thoroughly examine the Army's methods and institutions and publish a report. This committee was composed of some of the leading business and public men of England, headed by Sir Wilfred Lawson. They examined the books of the Army and studied the system and methods of the movement. They reported that all was entirely satisfactory and not only so, but that the movement and work was worthy of commendation. [10]

The report of this Committee, together with a demonstration of the work already accomplished, served to silence the critics to some extent, and public favor began to turn toward the movement. Since that period the Army has had, generally speaking, the support of the press and many of the leading men throughout the world, a support which it has not been slow to recognize, or to utilize. For instance, about this time, we find the following appeal issued through the English press:

"From personal witness or credible report of what General Booth has done with the funds entrusted to him for the Social Scheme which he laid before the country eighteen months ago, we think it would be a serious evil if the great task which he has undertaken should be crippled by lack of help during the next four months. We therefore venture to recommend his work to the generous support of all, who feel the necessity for some serious and concentrated effort to grapple with the needs of the most wretched and destitute, who have so long been the despair of our legislation and our philanthropy."

This appeal was signed by the Earl of Aberdeen, who was then Governor-General of Canada, and fifteen other men and women of international reputation. As an example of the attitude of the press, we find the London Daily Telegraph, in the midst of a long editorial entitled, "The General's Triumph," saying, "There is no question about it, the General has become popular. He has justified himself by results. We are told he has not shown the way out, but few have done so much to let the light in, and to bring with it life and healing." [11] Since the publication of "In Darkest England" in 1890, the social work of the Army has been extended, and has grown very rapidly. [12]

In connection with this rapid growth, the social phase of the movement has tended to eclipse the spiritual in the public eye. The Army has taken advantage of this to advertise its advancement along all lines, and there is reason for believing that the public support of the whole movement, both social and spiritual, at the present time, is largely due to this advertising. [13] In any case, the social work of the Army is a movement large enough to justify the interest of the public, and the extensive study of every student of practical social economy.

FOOTNOTES:

[2] "Social Relief Work of the Salvation Army in the U. S.," p. 5.

[3] "Life of William Booth," p. 57.

[4] "Social Relief Work of the S. A. in the U. S."

[5] "Sesame and Lillies," p. 101. Cf. also "The New Movement in Charity," Am. Jour. Soc. III, p. 596.

[6] "In Darkest England," pp. 85-87.

[7] Ibid., preface.

[8] Ibid., p. 15.

[9] "Social Diseases and Worse Remedies."

[10] "The committee of 1902 which inquired into certain aspects of the Darkest England Scheme two years after its initiation, were careful to state that they did not enter upon any consideration of the many economic questions affecting the maintenance of the system sought to be carried out." (The Salvation Army and the Public, p. 121.)

[11] "London Daily Telegraph," July 6, 1904.

[12] In fifteen years, from 1890 to 1905, the social work grew from a few small scattered institutions, to 687 institutions, many of which alone would have greater accommodation than the total in 1890.

[13] See "The S. A. and the Public," ch. 3.

CHAPTER I.

The Salvation Army Industrial Department.

Originally the work now known as the Industrial Work was handled with and under the same management as the Social Work, but as the movement grew, the Industrial Work branched out and finally became separate in operation and management, the name "Social Department" being retained for the hotel work only.

The Industrial Department itself may be divided into three sections, all under the same management. These are The Industrial Home, The Industrial Store and The Industrial Colony. The object of the work embraced in these three divisions as stated in the prospectus sent out by the Army two years ago is:

"One of the most difficult problems that has confronted the Salvation Army has been the finding of employment for out-of-works and human derelicts in our cities. A system has been gradually organized by which this human waste is employed in collecting the material waste of the city. This latter has been sorted, sifted and sold, and temporary employment thus afforded to thousands of stranded persons, who have thus been tided over periods of distress, relieved of immediate suffering, saved from the stigma of paupers, assured of human sympathy, and given a new start in life." [14]

After a careful review of the various divisions of this work, above mentioned, we shall consider whether the object is being attained, and of what value the work done is to society.

In the formation of the Industrial Home the ideal building and situation cannot always be secured; hence there are differences in the planning and disposition of the different homes. The general plan, however, is to have a three or four-story building fitted up as follows: On the ground floor is a space where the wagons filled with waste materials can unload, a large room where furniture can be repaired and stored (unless this is done in the basement below), an office, and another large room to be used for a retail store. On the second floor is the sorting room, and adjoining or connected with it is the baling room, where such stuff as paper, rags and excelsior is pressed, ready to be taken away. On this floor, too, is to be found the kitchen, the dining room and the reading room. On the third floor are situated the dormitories and sleeping rooms. This plan is often varied. Sometimes there is a basement and only one or two stories above. Sometimes, as in the Forty-eighth Street home in New York, there are six or seven stories, and sometimes, as in one home in Chicago, the sleeping and living quarters of the men are entirely separate from the warehouse where they work, possibly some blocks away. The kitchen is nearly always found to be large and furnished with a good range and other facilities. The dining room contains long, plain tables, set so that the men can sit on both sides. The dishes are of thick, strong ware. The food is plain but good. Everything from the floor to the dishes is usually clean.

The sleeping rooms are of two kinds, individual rooms and dormitories. Those men who are of a better rank, that is, those who have been working long, or who are doing a higher grade of work, and those who have "boss" positions, occupy the separate rooms; while the general class of workers sleep in the dormitories. When it comes to the question of pure air, considerable difficulty arises. Some of the separate rooms have no outside window, though the partitions between the rooms rise only to a certain height, thus giving common air to the whole floor. Even where good ventilation facilities exist, it seems difficult to make the men keep the windows open. As regards ventilation, however, the industrial homes are, as a rule, better than the lower class workingman's hotels, and are improving in this respect. The beds are iron, single beds. The bed clothing and the rooms themselves are clean and fumigated regularly.

A reading room is also provided where daily papers and popular magazines are kept, and where the men may write. In some cases, a smoking room adjoins. Meetings of a devotional character, to which the men may come or not as they see fit, are often held in the reading room.

The support that renders the industrial home possible is the waste product of the city. This material is rubbish of all kinds imaginable. In connection with each industrial plant are kept a number of horses and wagons, mostly one-horse wagons. Each driver of a wagon has a definite route to cover regularly. Passing over his route, he collects everything of which people are glad to be rid. Waste paper, old clothes, old furniture, and the like, are the principal articles he collects. Many good people, persuaded of the good work the Army is doing, save up their store of odds and ends until the Army wagon shall call, often giving things away which they would not have thrown away or given any one else, unless it would be to sell them to an old-clothes man. The driver returns with his load to the warehouse. From his wagon the material is conveyed by means of an elevator to the sorting room in the second story, whence the greater quantity goes at once to the baling machine in the form of waste paper. Any articles that may be of use, such as shoes, clothing of any kind, books, crockery-ware, bottles, pots, kettles, etc., are placed in their respective bins and finally, repaired, find their way to the retail store. Heavy articles, such as stoves and furniture, do not go up in the elevator, but are retained on the first floor, where they go, first to the repairing and storage room, and then out to the stores. The paper and rags, when baled, are sold to the nearest paper mill for a good price. Some idea of the amount of this class of material may be gained from the fact that the average amount of paper sold by the Industrial Department in the United States is about 2,500 tons per month.

In England and other countries this work has not assumed such large proportions, but there is some difference between the workings of the industrial plant in the City of London and in New York. For instance, at the Salvation Army plant on Hanbury Street, Whitechapel, London, we found, in 1906, a planing mill, a paint and furniture shop, a mattress factory, and a sawmill and cabinet shop. This place had employment for ninety men, of whom twelve were regularly employed and the remainder were transients. The regular employees were paid at a union rate of wages. The men of this industrial plant lived some distance away on Quaker Street, having possession of part of the Salvation Army shelter or hotel there, the total accommodation of which was two hundred and forty. Again, in a different part of the city, over near Deptford, was a wood yard with good machinery, run by electricity, which employed anywhere from sixty to seventy men making kindling wood. On the other hand, at the "Spa Road Elevator," was a plant almost identical with the industrial plants in the United States, where were shipped out an average of 100 pounds of paper every week and several tons of rags in addition, and where was accommodation for some two hundred men.

Branching out from the main industrial plant are nearly always to be found large stores. These are Salvation Army retail stores. These stores are found in the poorest sections of the city, and are patronized by the poorest class. Articles of all descriptions may be purchased here at a very low figure. In each store is a furniture department; a clothing department for men, women and children; a toy department; a department for stoves, pots, etc., and sometimes other departments varying with the size of the store. It is possible, thus, for a poor family moving into the neighborhood to completely furnish themselves and their home from Salvation Army stores at a cost of often less than one-half of what they would pay elsewhere. Each store has a definite connection with the central industrial plant, from which it receives its supplies, its workers and its government, for the stores are merely branches of the central work, and all are under the same general management.

An interesting feature lies in an examination of the labor which is employed. From the cases given at the end of the chapter, it will be seen that it consists of all kinds, classes and nationalities, who, through their own recklessness, or by unfortunate circumstances, have fallen into want. A man willing to work comes to the Army in want of food and shelter, and the Army happens to have accommodation for him. He may go to one of the men's hotels or to the industrial home, or to the central agency of the Army. In any case he will probably be interviewed by an officer specially detailed for the purpose, who will be able to

decide in short time what his needs are, and what can be done for him. He may be sent out at once to take some position secured through the employment bureau; he may be sent to the hotel with the understanding that, after being fed and cared for, he will be given an opportunity to pay for it in work; or he may be sent straight to the industrial home. In any case, if possible, he is put to work. He may be in a weak condition physically or mentally, or both, but even then, he can often do something; such, for example, as picking over paper and rags in the sorting room.
Meanwhile, he is being fed and housed. If he means well and works earnestly, he is soon able to do some other grade of work. He may have had technical knowledge which will help him. In a few days, possibly, a call is made to the employment bureau, which is maintained in conjunction with each home or group of homes, for a man to fill some position. If suitable, this man may be sent out to take it. On the other hand, he may be retained in the home and employed permanently as a driver on one of the wagons, or as overseer and instructor in one of the rooms, or he may be sent out as assistant to one of the stores, and, in time, he may be given charge of a store. When the men first come to the home, they receive board and clothing and some remuneration, although very slight. If they continue to work at the home, they are paid wages ranging from $1.00 per week up to $4.00 or $5.00 per week, besides board and lodging in the United States, and from 1s. to 9s. in England.

When a man is able, but is lazy and not willing to work, he is turned out. It is well known to those who have studied the question, that there are a large number of such men, but this class does not apply for help as often as it might to the Army, as it soon learns the uselessness of so doing. The officers become quite adept in seeing these men in their true colors. On the other hand, if a man drops into bad habits and goes off on a spree after he has been helped, he will be taken in again afterwards, and this is continued within reason. Much of the labor employed is a surface and floating population, the result of season and periodic work in connection with so many of our industries, and the men are just tided over a hard time in their experiences. This class is larger sometimes than at others, but is always in evidence. Another class, however, consists of the men who have fallen through their own recklessness and bad habits. Some of these men are sent out to positions which they fill creditably, and finally rise as high or higher than they were before. Naturally, the Army makes as much as possible out of these cases for the purpose of advertisement. Owing to evident difficulties, it is impossible to ascertain just what percentage there is of this class among the total number helped, or what percentage of this class itself is successfully aided. The industrial work itself, as a paying business, is developing so fast that a constantly increasing number of men are permanently retained and used as regular employees, being paid regular wages.

When we come to the industrial colony, we find it entirely different from the farm colony, where families are sent to settle upon the land in tracts of say twenty acres per family. The industrial colony is managed like a large farm with many laborers, all under one central head. The original idea was to graduate men from the city plants to the industrial colonies and thence to the farm colonies, but the Army has had difficulty in maintaining its colonies at all, and, as a result, no regular system has been followed. A large proportion of the men on the industrial colony are single, whereas, as will be seen, families are needed for the farm colonies. Again, many of these men are not the kind who will succeed on the farm colony. Sometimes, too, they have not been through the city plant, and sometimes they are men sent directly from the city to get them out of temptations which are too strong for them.

The best example of an industrial colony is the one at Hadleigh, about thirty miles from London, England. This colony has an area of about 3,000 acres. One thousand acres is almost useless now; and when taken by the Army in 1890, the whole consisted of almost worthless land, some of which, as a result of constant labor and fertilization, has been transformed into reasonably good land. A great draw-back and a great expense has been the lack of water, now partially supplied by two artesian wells, the cheaper of which cost over $20,000.00. [15] The population varies from 300 to 700. [16] In 1898, 775 men were admitted to the colony. Out of this number, 193 left after a short residence before they could be influenced for good; 47 were discharged as incorrigible, and 309 graduated, obtaining situations or being restored to their friends. [17] There are three classes received at the colony:

1. Those sent by the Army agencies.

2. Those sent by poor law authorities who pay from 5s. to 10s. per week for periods of from three to twelve months for their maintenance.

3. Special cases sent by philanthropic societies, or by relatives or others. [18]

Another division is made into four classes, thus:

1. Those coming and passing off in a month, not being regular colonists.

2. Those averaging nine months on the colony, and called colonists.

3. Picked men from the second class, who are made employees.

4. Employees hired in the neighborhood for specific purposes. [19]

The proportion of each, according to either specification, is such a variable quantity that nothing can be determined satisfactorily. According to one officer's statement, about one in every five is considered an employee. [20] In the winter of 1903-4, 209 men were sent to Hadleigh and supported there by a special fund, called "The Mansion House Fund for the Relief of the London Unemployed." [21] Out of the class sent by the Army agencies to the colony, a certain number are sent out as emigrants to Canada. For instance, in 1905, 41 were sent out, and in 1906, 58. The party of 58 was composed of five Irishmen, one Welshman, three Scotchmen, and forty-nine Englishmen. These men go to work on different farms in Canada, and some sent out in previous years now have homesteads there. In the colony there are five departments, viz.: the market garden, the brick-making department, the dairy department together with the piggery, the poultry department, and the Inebriate's Home. There is also a store which has an income of $1,000.00 a month. The market garden is one of the best industries, most of the produce being sold in the town of Southend, four miles distant. In the busy season, as many as 100 workers are found in this department. There are four large conservatories, especially for tomatoes and flowers. A good many potatoes are raised, and there is a good deal of land in berries and orchard. There are three brick-yards with the latest improved kilns and machinery. These yards have been a very heavy expense and have not been satisfactory. For instance, in 1898, the year's sale of bricks amounted to £4717, while the expenditure of this department was £5563, this latter sum including the expense of repairing the drying fields, which that year were injured by a flood. [22] In the dairy department about twenty-five head of cattle provide the colony with milk and butter, while sometimes milk is sold at Southend. In the piggery the number of hogs runs from 200 to 500. The poultry department is given over to prize poultry breeding and has been successful in winning some noted prizes. The Inebriate's Home is licensed for twenty male inebriates who are charged from 25s. to 30s. per week. Between 60% and 70% are stated to be reclaimed after an average period of eight months' treatment. In addition to these departments it might be noted that there is a school on the colony with an attendance of 100, some of whom come from outside the colony, and a good sized hall, seating about 400, where gatherings are held for social and religious purposes.

For the feeding and lodging of the colonists, large preparations are made. They are graded according to their position in the colony, and an opportunity is given them to rise from the lower to the higher grades. The superintendent stated that this plan was found useful in stimulating ambition. There are two dormitories, both clean and well-kept, but the higher grade with better bedding and surroundings than the lower. This grading system is also maintained in the dining room, the higher grade of colonists being served with better food than the lower. Everything around the buildings is well-kept and orderly, and the general moral atmosphere of the colony seems to be healthful and up-lifting.

The industrial colony at Ft. Herrick, near Cleveland, Ohio, differs in many ways from the one at Hadleigh, and doubtless has been instrumental in aiding a good number of outcast and fallen men, but it has been such a burden financially, and such an unsolved problem in many ways, that it may be considered a failure. The reason for its failure is not so much bad management as lack of foresight on the part of those choosing the site. The site is in no sense suitable for a colony, the soil being unfit for intensive farming. Probably the best work done there has been the reformation of drunkards, a work in which, according to reports, the colony has been eminently successful. [23]

Coming now to the management of the Industrial Department in the United States, we find that it is an up-to-date business enterprise. The department is controlled by a corporation called "The Salvation Army Industrial Homes Co." already referred to in our introduction. [24] The management of the company is in the hands of the Army. [25] Under this central authority, we find the United States divided into three districts; the eastern district, with headquarters at New York; the central district with headquarters at Cleveland, and the western district with headquarters at Chicago. Each one of these districts has at its head a social secretary, and under him are the different officers in charge of the respective plants. Generally speaking, each local officer is supreme in his individual plant. He can adopt methods and means to suit the environment of his district, provided always that his methods mean success. There are no iron-clad rules to hold him in check beyond a system of bookkeeping and of making out detailed reports, which must be sent to headquarters. When about to engage in some new venture, however, such as securing a new location for his plant, opening up a store, or renting or purchasing new property, he must refer the project to his superior officer, before undertaking it. The local officer in charge has trusted employees under him, such as a warehouse boss, a kitchen boss, and stable boss, etc., each of whom is responsible to the officer for his department.

Although present to some extent in other countries the special field of the industrial work is the United States. The growth in this country during the recent years has been great. In 1896 there were no regular industrial homes; in 1904 there were 49 industrial institutions, and in control of these 49 institutions, there were 70 Army officers and 820 regular employees. The accommodation was about 1,100. During one month there were 225 cases that were considered unsatisfactory. There were 239 horses and wagons in daily use. About 1,000 tons of paper were baled and sold per month. Contrast this with the year 1907. In this year there were 84 officers engaged in these institutions and over 1,200 regular employees. There was accommodation for 1,651 men. The unsatisfactory cases for the year amounted to 1,389. There were 460 horses and wagons in daily use. An average of 2,500 tons of paper was sold each month. 16,875 men were placed in outside positions during the year. No large city in the United States is without this industrial work, and it is to be expected that, within a few years, there will be no city in the country with a population of 100,000 that does not have an industrial home, and that many cities with a smaller population will have one also. Already there are several cities with a population of less than 50,000 that have promising industrial plants. In London, the growth has not been so rapid, and the industrial institutions are run at a loss to the Army, but there are about eight industrial plants in that city, and others are to be found in other large cities of England.

We come now to the question of the value of the Salvation Army industrial work to society. From the preceding brief outline of the methods, material, labor, management and extent of the industrial work, it will be seen that it is a movement, unrestricted in scope, with an unlimited field of development as an economic enterprise. In certain fields where the Army is active, its work is considered of little or no value; but as a result of our investigation into this particular field, the conclusion is reached that, with the exception of the industrial colonies, it is a practical, social work, of value to society.

We make an exception of the industrial colonies because we do not consider that the two experiments already tried by the Army justify their own continuance or the starting of other similar colonies. The reference here is to Fort Herrick in Ohio, and the Hadleigh Colony, near London. These colonies have necessitated a continual sinking of funds contributed by the charitable public, and the return does not justify their expense. The Army should realize this, and admit the fact, instead of drawing wool over the eyes of the ignorant public by the constant reiteration of "the great work done at Hadleigh and Fort Herrick." It looks as though the organization was afraid that the infallibility and sanctity of General Booth's pet scheme would be seriously impaired, if the public should discover that any part of that scheme was a mistake and an unfortunate experiment, and that, for this reason, it has continued to expend much money on it, which might have been turned to better advantage in connection with other parts of General Booth's plan. These colonies are object lessons showing what is unwise to attempt, rather than what can be done. The Army has no need to be ashamed of having made a mistake, and its usefulness along other lines is sufficient to maintain its reputation in spite of the failure of its industrial colonies. There is no need of the industrial colony anyway. The object in view is either to tide workless men over a period of hard times and misfortune, or to restore manhood where evil habits and recklessness have destroyed it, and this can be done and is being done by means of the city industrial work without the aid of the colony. As regards the work of reforming the inebriate, in which the industrial colonies have had some success, that could be carried on without the great expense of a regular colony.

The moral field of the city industrial work derives support from the relation of its management to the spiritual work and influence of the Army. The influence and spirit of the whole organization runs to a certain extent through every branch of its varied developments. This influence cannot be described by comparative means. The spirit, somewhat unique in itself, runs through everything, a spirit which is a mixture and blending of love, gratitude, service and patience. While we think that, in the tendency of this branch to become a business enterprise, there is a considerable decrease in the influence just described, it still has great power. The officers and employees now engaged in this work were themselves not long since outcasts in society. Many of them had despaired of ever making a success of life and were simply drifting. But a helping hand had been stretched out to them, hope had been imparted and new ideals had been placed before them. They might even yet be men, wear decent clothes, stand up straight and look their fellow men in the eye! What wonder that the decent clothes to which they looked forward turned out to be the uniform of the organization which had picked them up from the gutter! What wonder they felt an eternal debt of gratitude toward that organization! While this is not a true expression of their attitude in every case, and while there are some who hold their positions simply because they can get no better, loyalty to the work exists in enough instances to create a distinct moral atmosphere. The men wish to make a success of their new work; they wish to see the Army advance, and to do this they feel that it is essential that the same moral influence which enabled them to become men should be continued. This influence moves almost unconsciously among the industrial plants. For instance, we do not find here the tendency to obscenity which we find in any ordinary factory or workshop. Environment in these plants is all-powerful as an uplifting condition. Cleanliness is encouraged in the dormitory and kitchen. Respectful attention is paid at meals while grace is being said. The reading room is frequented, while the occasional meetings held are sometimes well attended and sometimes not, according to the attraction. The emotional religious element is a great deal in evidence, though not so much as in other departments of the Army. In any case, the element of hope and ambition, which often arises within these social outcasts, making them men once more, is to be considered a great moral asset. The moral influence is due more to the personality of those in charge than to anything else. A large number of the managers have served in connection with the Army's spiritual work and have the desire, as they would tell you, to see every man under them "saved," not only in a moral and social sense, but "saved" in accordance with the Army's special significance of that term. [26] While the Army's special idea of salvation may have no value in itself, still if the emotional element assists in the moral and social salvation of individuals, we have no reason for not tolerating it unless it has evil effects of real importance. Such effects, however, tend to decrease, as the movement advances, and the education and enlightenment of the masses increase.

From an economic point of view, we believe that the work of the Industrial Department has been successful. We have seen that large numbers of men, who are out of work, are taken in by this department and kept for a number of weeks or months, and that, during this time, besides making their own support, and gaining in efficiency, in many cases, they are able to return to a more important part in production. Let us see what this means. While these men are out of work, they are not producing anything. They are idle, and thus a loss to the community. In addition, they are fast losing any potential ability for production, which they have had. But they now become producers, a gain to the community, and their potential ability for production is at least conserved if not increased. Secondly, out-of-work men are a burden on the community. While they continue to live without employment, they must be supported in some way or other by private or public charity, and they form a great item of expense to the community. But in the hands of the Industrial Department, they cease being an expense to the public and become to some extent a gain. Thirdly, some of these men are in danger of becoming members of pseudo-social and anti-social classes; it is from them that the pauper and criminal classes gain recruits. But through the elevating environment of this branch of the Army's work, their character is affected, and they are raised to a higher level. In this way then, in successful cases, the worthless men become workmen. Worthless men are changed into economic assets. The dependents become independent. Working by means of the laws of environment and association, the Army elevates the degenerate from a pseudo-social and anti-social class to a higher level and to social position. Where individuality was lost, independence of character reasserts itself.

Let us consider in detail some of the advantages connected with this form of practical philanthropy. One advantage is, that once started, the work continues and increases without further expenditure on the part of the charitably disposed public beyond the giving away of things for which they have no further use. This is so because the Army here in its work becomes an efficient producer and creates articles which have market value. Leaving all charity alone, the work is paying and more than self-supporting, and thus in a short time will be reimbursed with all the money which was necessary to initiate it. In nearly every city in which the work was started, rented property soon gives place to property owned by the Army and poor ill-suited buildings, to up-to-date structures built for the purpose. An example of this is to be found in the history of the 48th Street Industrial Home in New York City which is briefly described, in the examples given at the end of this chapter. [27] That the entire work has grown self-supporting in the United States is shown by the fact that last year, 1907, there was a net gain of $21,000, after the interest on the loans and investments had been paid. If a home does not show signs of being successful financially, its location will be changed or it will be discontinued. [28]

Another advantage lies in the fact that men who were socially dependent are made self-supporting. We should place emphasis on the effect on the man himself as well as on the community. We saw how these men were given to understand that they were earning their own livelihood and were not recipients of charity, and how they were encouraged by the receipt of wages, to be increased as their productiveness increased. The relief given is true relief in that the man earns it himself and realizes this fact, and because, along with this realization, comes a return of manhood and independence. Of course if men have lost all manhood and have no desire to be independent, but simply to live as easily as possible on what may be given them, the above is not the result; but few such get into the industrial homes, as they know better and have no wish to work as these men do, and if they get in temporarily, they are soon sorted out. Thus it cannot be said of these homes as is said of many institutions, that they pauperize men in place of helping them. The institution that makes men work for everything they get and provides some sort of channel for their ambition, maintaining itself meanwhile as a paying concern, is not pauperizing in its tendency.

Still another advantage of this work is found in the saving of the community's funds. Of late years, more and more, the principle has been advanced and brought before the public, that the starving and unemployed are to be cared for in some way, and we are willing to tax ourselves to provide for this. As far back as the census of 1890, we find that the United States spent annually $40,000,000 in charities and over $12,000,000 in penal and reformatory institutions. Probably the total expenditure for these two objects to-day would be nearer $60,000,000 annually. What percentage of this $60,000,000 would go to the class of people aided by the Army industrial work would be hard to ascertain or approximate, but there is room for a great extension of this kind of work, and the Army's efforts are most suggestive. In some of the European countries, especially Germany, many helpful experiments along this line are in progress, but conditions in the United States are vastly different. In any case social economists are agreed that vast sums are spent annually in our country to little or no purpose from the point of view of social relief. In the year 1907, 8,696 men were cared for in the United States industrial homes of the Army. This means just that amount of saving to the nation that it would have cost the regular municipal and state charities to have dealt with these 8,696 men, since these men were aided by a self-supporting organization and paid for their own support. This work, then, if carried far enough, would effect quite a saving of taxes.

But along with advantages there may be disadvantages. Some objections have been raised to this branch of the Army's work. For instance, it is stated that industries entered into by the Army tend to hurt economic conditions with regard to both wages and prices. [29] With regard to wages it is urged that the Army will keep for its industries, workers in constraint of one kind or another, paying them a lower wage than the same workers could procure outside, and thus lowering the wages in the respective industries. We do not consider this objection a strong one. Let us forget for the present the philanthropic side of the industrial work, and look on it as a distinctly economic enterprise, as a factor of production. We think it quite likely that a manager, anxious above everything else to make his institution a financial success, would make an endeavor to keep as long as possible, and at as low wages as possible, men who could receive more on the outside. He might even try to retain men for whom he could secure better positions through the employment bureau, if he needed their services, and times were so good that no other applicant offered to take their place, but this he could not succeed in doing to any serious extent; for, in the first place, the restraint exercised over the men is very slight, and secondly, if the men could secure better wages, it would not be long before they found it out and left the home voluntarily. It would be just the same as in any industry in which most of the workers are ignorant. They would remain under low wages just as long as their ignorance and lack of initiative would allow, but sooner or later the relatively able man would seek the best wage. Hence the able man would seek the best wage, and his place would be taken by one, possibly morally and physically unable to procure any wage, or, in other words, belonging to the unemployable class. If it should come to the point of the Army's hiring able men to carry on the work without aiding the outcasts, it must compete in the market for them and pay the market price. The only real danger would lie in the Army's industrial work securing a strong enough position in some industry to be able to dictate terms to labor in an industry, but this is so unlikely as to be almost irrelevant and even in such an almost inconceivable case, the danger would be only temporary. Labor would still be able to drift sufficiently to another agency, not controlled by the Army and thus bring up wages again. This is the more true in that any industry, in which the Army engages, must of necessity be one in which unskilled labor is competent. [30] In addition to this, from personal investigation, we can state that a large part of the labor employed in these plants of the Army is at any rate temporarily inefficient labor and would not have much chance in securing employment elsewhere. Finally, though considered a charitable work, this branch of the army is, as already stated, a corporation, a business enterprise financed by investors who receive interest on their investments; hence, to the same extent that it is a financial enterprise, like other such enterprises, it will be governed by the rate of wages. [31]

Another objection has been raised by critics, to the effect that the Army, through its industry, enters into competition with existing firms and companies to the harm of the latter. [32] For instance they urge that in the case of those engaged in second-hand goods and salvage, who are able to make a profit by buying their material, the army enters into an unfair competition, when it takes such material, given in charity, and sells at a lower figure. In so far as the army does undersell others this objection is valid, and we have no doubt that in some cases such is the truth. Doubtless some individuals and firms have been hurt in their business by this under-selling. For instance, in Chicago, the Army has nine retail stores situated in the poorer districts, doing a big business in second hand goods. In addition to those goods it sends into the retail trade, it sells hundreds of tons of paper and rags annually. This must have some effect on others engaged in this business. However, the Army itself sometimes pays for its material and does not often undersell. [33] But there is another side to this question of underselling. Naturally the tendency is to get as much as possible for its goods, and provided there is a market, the army would seek to obtain just as much as any one else in the business. It now falls back on a question of supply and demand. The only way in which the price would be lowered by the Salvation Army would be by an increase of supply. Doubtless the supply of these goods is increased by the thorough work of the Army agents, and, to such an extent, its entrance into this field would tend to lower prices. However, in the leading salvage industries of the army, the increase in supply does no more than offset the increase in demand. The amount of displacement of the salvage and allied industries due to the competition of the army at present would not seem to be much, although of course it is difficult to get any exact figures along this line.

Looking at the Salvation Army retail store as a form of relief, another question arises as to whether the opportunity given to the residents of the district to get things at the Salvation Army's store cheaper than elsewhere interferes with the standard of living. By the standard of living we mean the scale or measure of comfort and satisfaction which a person or a community of persons regards as indispensable to happiness. [34] This would differ in the case of different persons and classes and communities, but progress demands that the standard should never be lowered, but should always be raised, in accord with increasing enlightenment and education.

"It is only," says Dr. Devine, "when individuals or individual families for personal or exceptional or temporary reasons fall below the standard, that charitable assistance can effectively intervene. In other words, as has been pointed out in other connections, the relieving policy cannot be made to raise the general standard of living, but it should be so established as not to depress it" [35].

Here, then, the point is, whether those who are otherwise able to come up to the standard of living in a given community take advantage of this form of charity, or whether the customers of the Salvation Army's stores are living below that standard. To just the extent that the former is true, this part of the work would be pauperizing and retrogressive, but we do not consider the former to be true. Naturally, we have no statistics on this point, but speaking from general observation, we should say that the customers of these stores are needy poor, who are living below the standard, and hence, the store is a boon to them in aiding them toward a realization of that standard.

Let us now sum up our conclusions regarding the industrial work of the Army. Regarding the industrial colonies, we would say that, while doubtless responsible for good and reformation in certain cases, nevertheless, owing to their cost of maintenance and the fact that the work can be done without them, they are not a practical form of charity deserving the intelligent support of the public. Regarding the city industrial work, including the employment, amid a good environment, of men out of work, including also the turning of much otherwise waste matter into an economic good, and the assistance of deserving poor by means of second-hand stores, we would say that it is commendable and deserving of support. This latter conclusion is made in spite of three objections: first, that there is a tendency to lower wages, which objection we do not consider as important for reasons given; second, that underselling of certain commodities by the Army takes place, which objection we admit to a limited extent, and third, that the standard of living is interfered with, which objection we do not consider valid.

Examples of Men in the Army Industrial Homes.

These examples were collected by Mr. Jas. Ward at the two industrial homes situated on West 19th Street and West 48th Street, New York City, during the months of March and April, 1908. Mr. Ward worked right with the men whose cases are given here, and slept in the homes, thus being with them night and day. The home on West 19th Street was an old milk depot rented temporarily by the Army to aid the unemployed during the winter, and had accommodation for two hundred men. Everything was very crude. The men slept on the floor, some without blankets. They were required to work from three to five hours every day, and during the rest of the day, they were allowed to go out and seek for work. The best of these men were drafted out to fill the vacancies in the regular industrial homes of the Army as they occurred. On the other hand, the home on West 48th Street was and is one of the Army's best homes, built for the purpose by the Army in 1907, at a cost of $130,000.00. Everything here is arranged for comfort and cleanliness. The dormitory is of the best, with good ventilation and other sanitary conditions. It is a seven-story building, and has accommodation for one hundred and seventy-five men. Twenty-two wagons are sent out from this home every day. In every way it is a contrast with the West 19th Street home, hence the examples will show some difference, according to which home they refer.

No. 1.

Born in Ireland. Thirty-eight years old. Single. Had no trade. Had worked on a farm in Ireland. Had been in this country fourteen years and had worked somewhat on a farm in this country. Had been out of work two months. Lost his position through an accident and spent three weeks in the hospital. Had since been in the Army Industrial Home for five weeks, and was growing stronger. His appearance was very good.

No. 2.

Born in France. Thirty-five years old. Single. Had people in France but never heard from them. Had no trade. Out of work all winter. Worked on a farm a little in France. In this country fifteen years. Several charitable societies had helped him and he had been in the Industrial Home eight days. The Army gave him clothing and shoes. He looked like a drinking man, but otherwise capable.

No. 3.

Born in Italy. Thirty years old. Married. Had wife in Italy. Left there two years ago, and said he was going to send for his wife when he got the money. He had worked on a farm in Italy, and had worked at different trades in this country. Had been out of work nine weeks. Had been in the

Industrial Home two days. Spoke good English. Looked dirty and without much intelligence.

No. 4.

Born in South Carolina. Twenty-three years old. Single. Trade of a plumber. Left his people five months ago and came to New York. Soon spent his money and could find no work. Had been in the Industrial Home three weeks. Said he was going home as soon as he could get the money. Never worked on a farm. Looked capable.

No. 5.

Born in Germany. Forty-two years old. Single. Had been in this country twenty-five years and had followed the water nearly all the time. Got in a fight on the Bowery six months ago and spent five months in jail. Since coming out, he had had odd jobs, and had been in the Industrial Home about two weeks. Looked shiftless and dissipated.

No. 6.

Born in Denver, Colo. American parents. Twenty-six years old. Single. Had people in Philadelphia who did not help him. Machinist by trade. Belonged to the union in Philadelphia. Out of work ten weeks. Said he had $100.00 but it did not last long. Had been in the Industrial Home two days and expected work shortly. Appearance was very good.

No. 7.

Born in Ireland. Forty years old. Married. Had left his family. Had no trade. In this country eight years. Never worked in the country. Out of work all winter. Spent three weeks in the hospital. Said he had consumption. Had been in the Industrial Home four days. Looked very feeble but not dissipated.

No. 8.

Born in New York. American parents. Twenty-six years old. Single. People lived in New York, but he had not lived with them for three years. Had no trade. Had travelled a little. Said he did not like hard work. Had been in the Industrial Home two weeks. The Army gave him clothing and shoes. Said the missions helped him. Expected to wander West when the weather got warm. Looked like a tramp. Never worked in the country.

No. 9.

Born in San Francisco. German parents. Fifty-eight years old. Single. Had no trade. Said he had beaten his way all around the world. Had not worked all winter. In the Industrial Home ten days. Looked shiftless and dissipated. Never worked in the country.

No. 10.

Born in Maine. English parents. Twenty-four years old. Single. Had people in Maine with whom he quarreled. Had no trade. Out of work for four months. In the Industrial Home one week. Never worked on a farm, but had worked in the woods. Did not drink. Looked like a capable man.

No. 11.

Born in Philadelphia. Irish parents. Twenty-six years old. Single. People in Philadelphia who helped him sometimes. Had no trade. Had wandered a good deal. Out of work three months. Said he drank whenever he could get liquor. Expected to go home shortly. Had been in the Industrial Home three days. Looked very shiftless and dissipated.

No. 12.

Born in Ireland. Forty-two years old. Single. Had two sisters in Brooklyn who were poor. In this country eighteen years. Had no regular trade but worked in hotels as porter. Out of work five months. Worked on a farm a good deal in Ireland. Looked like a vagrant.

No. 13.

Born in New York. American parents. Twenty-two years old. Single. Said he was a truck driver. Had been out of work one month. Drank sometimes. Had been in the Industrial Home four days. Expected to leave New York as soon as the weather became warmer. Looked very wild.

No. 14.

Born in Vermont. Mother Irish. Father German. Thirty-two years old. Single. He wrote to his people but they did not help him. Had travelled around a good deal. Had no trade. Said he "got saved" in a mission and they kept him all winter. He said every time he got down, he went to the missions and stayed as long as he could. Had been in the Industrial Home nine days. Had worked on a farm a little. Looked like a vagrant.

No. 15.

Born in London. Twenty-two years old. Single. Seaman by trade. Left his boat one month ago in New York and had done nothing since. Had been in the Industrial Home two weeks and hoped to work his way back to England shortly. His appearance was very good.

No. 16.

Born in New York. American parents. About thirty-five years old. Single. Brick-layer by trade. Did not belong to the union. Out of work four months. Said he had been to every city in the United States and had travelled on freight trains quite often. Looked like a tramp.

No. 17.

Born in Reading, Penna. American parents. Forty years old. Married. Wife dead. One child living with his sister in Pennsylvania. Carpenter by trade. Did not belong to the union. Had been out of work all winter. All his tools were in pawn. The Army had been helping him at times. Said he had to leave his child on account of not working. He looked like a very hard drinker. Had never worked in the country.

No. 18.

Born in Albany, N. Y. American parents. Thirty-five years old. Single. Quarrelled with his people. Had not been home for ten years. Had no trade. Out of work all winter. The missions and the Army had helped him a good deal. Had been in the Industrial Home three days. Never worked in the country. Looked dissipated.

No. 19.

Born in Ireland. Thirty years old. Single. Had people in Ireland who were poor. Came to this country eleven years ago. Had no trade. Out of work two months. Expected a position in Brooklyn the following week. Said he had $60.00 in the bank but lost his book and had to wait to get his money. Had been in the Industrial Home two days. His appearance was good.

No. 20.

Born in Jersey City. Italian parents. Twenty-five years old. Single. Quarrelled with his people. Said he had a stepmother and could not get along with her. Had been in New York five years working at everything. Had no trade. Out of work five months. Had saved some money, but it was all gone. Never worked in the country. In the Industrial Home five days. Said this was the first time he was ever down. Looked like a hopeful case.

No. 21.

Born in Philadelphia. Irish parents. Thirty-two years old. Married. His wife was working and had paid his board all winter, until he came to New York two weeks before on a freight train. Had been in the Industrial Home since, and expected to return to his wife. Carpet-weaver by trade and belonged to the union. Said he drank sometimes, but he looked like a hard drinker. Otherwise very good.

No. 22.

Born in Brooklyn. American parents. Thirty years old. Single. People lived in Brooklyn, but they did not have anything to do with him. Piano-finisher by trade. Did not belong to the union. Was in the army one year and deserted. Out of work three months. Came to New York two months ago. Spent all his money, $50.00, in two days. Had been in the Industrial Home two weeks. Said he was going to reform and get a steady job. Looked like a hard drinker but otherwise capable.

No. 23.

Born in Scranton, Penna. German parents. Fifty years old. Single. Had one sister and one brother at home, but he did not write them. Had no trade. Had travelled all over the United States. Seemed to know a mission in every city. Never worked in the country. Had been in the Industrial Home some time, and said they made him work too hard. Looked like a vagrant.

No. 24.

Born in Springfield, Mass. American parents. Forty years old. Single. Had no trade. Had not worked for over a year. Had been in jail several times for riding freights. Never worked in the country. The missions and the Army had helped him this winter. Looked like a dissipated character.

No. 25.

Born in Germany. Twenty-five years old. Had people in Germany who were poor. Left home eight months ago and came to New York, with a little money. Had not worked since he left home. He spoke broken English. Had no trade. Did not drink much. Had been in the Industrial Home some time. Looked intelligent and capable. Never worked in the country.

No. 26.

Born in Ireland. Forty-five years old. Single. Had no trade. Had been in this country twenty years. Worked a good deal on a farm. Had wandered a good deal. He said the Army were good people and had helped him in different cities. Had been out of work two months. Looked shiftless.

No. 27.

Born in Greenwich, Conn. American parents. Twenty-seven years old. Single. Used to be in business with his father as a plumber in Greenwich, but quarrelled and had not been home for six years. Never worked on a farm. Looked intelligent but very wild. Said he could have anything he wanted at home, if he would leave the drink alone.

No. 28.

Born in Boston, Mass. Scotch parents. Fifty-three years old. Married. Divorced seven years ago. Brass-moulder by trade. Had belonged to the union but lost his membership through non-payment of dues. Out of work three months. He drank a good deal, but looked capable. Never worked in the country.

No. 29.

Born in Cleveland, O. American parents. Twenty-seven years old. Single. Had no regular trade. Made a business of following fairs as a fakir. Never worked in the country. Said the missions and the Army had helped him a good deal this winter. He also spent several nights in the city lodging house. Looked capable but a little dissipated.

No. 30.

Born in Yonkers, N. Y. American parents. Thirty-six years old. Single. Had no trade. Had not worked all winter. Was in the Industrial Home for the fourth time this winter. The missions had helped him. Never worked in the country. Looked like a vagrant.

No. 31.

Born in Germany. Forty years old. Single. Had no trade. Out of work two months. The Army gave him clothing. Had been in the Industrial Home several days. Never stayed in one place very long. Never worked in the country. Looked like a vagrant.

No. 32.

Born in New York. American parents. Thirty-five years old. Single. Had no people, except one brother who was in the West. Had no trade. Out of work four months. Had been in the Industrial Home one week. Never worked in the country. Said when he had money he gambled and played the races. Looked intelligent and capable.

No. 33.

Born in Ireland. Forty five years old. Married. Evidently had left his family. Had no regular trade. Had followed the water a good deal and worked along the docks. Had nothing steady for three months. Was in the Industrial Home for the second time this winter. Worked in the country about two years. Said when the weather got warm he was going to the country. Looked ignorant and dissipated.

No. 34.

Born in New York. American parents. Thirty years old. Single. Trade of a shoe-maker, but he had not worked at it for nearly two years. Out of work three months. Worked in the country a little. Appearance very good.

No. 35.

Born in Philadelphia. American parents. Forty years old. Married. Had buried his wife and three children. Had no trade but followed the circus as laborer. Never worked in the country. Had had no steady work for a year. The Army had been helping him for a month. He said he went on the drunk sometimes. Looked intelligent but in feeble health.

No. 36.

Born in Hungary. Twenty-nine years old. Single. Had people at home but did not write often. In this country eight years. Talked good English. Had no trade. Worked on a farm a good deal in Hungary. Had been in the Industrial Home four days. Looked very hopeful.

No. 37.

Born in Pittsfield, Mass. American parents. Twenty-one years old. Single. Had no trade. Had been in the Industrial Home three months. Was a trusted worker and received $2.50 a week, for driving one of the Army wagons. Never worked in the country. Looked like a respectable man.

No. 38.

Born in Ireland. Fifty-years old. Single. In this country twenty years. Had no trade. Had travelled around the world. Had been in the Industrial Home one month. Said he used to drink, but would never do it again. He was gray-haired and feeble. Never worked in the country.

No. 39.

Born in Ireland. Fifty-five years old. Single. Had no trade but followed the water a good deal. Out of work five months. Had been in the Industrial Home three weeks. Said the Army had helped him before. Looked like a vagrant.

No. 40.

Born in New York. Irish parents. Twenty-eight years old. Single. People lived in New York, but he had not lived home for several years. Quarrelled with his people because of drink. Had no trade. Worked one season in the country. Had been out of work two months. In the Industrial Home two weeks. The Army had fitted him out with clothing. Looked capable but dissipated.

No. 41.

Born in Germany. Thirty-seven years old. Married. Would not say anything about his family. In this country eleven years. Had no trade but followed the water as cook or waiter. Had been out of work all winter. The German Aid Society had helped him. Never worked in the country. Looked dissipated.

No. 42.

Born in England. Sixty-five years old. Married. Wife dead. Five children living, but they did not help him. Came to this country forty years ago. Bricklayer by trade. Belonged to the union, but said they did not help him. Had been out of work five months. Had been in the Industrial Home several times this winter. Looked old, gray-haired and feeble.

No. 43.

Born in New York. American parents. Twenty-five years old. Single. Had no trade. Quarrelled with his people three years ago and had not been home since. Never worked in the country. Had been in the Industrial Home four days. Looked quite capable.

No. 44.

Born in Germany. Twenty-nine years old. Single. Had people in Long Island who were poor. Had no trade, but followed the water a good deal. Out of work four months. In the Industrial Home five weeks. The Army gave him clothes. Said he drank a good deal. Never worked in the country. Looked intelligent but dissipated.

No. 45.

Born in Paterson, N. J. German parents. Twenty-five years old. Had people in Paterson but was ashamed to write to them. Had no trade. Had been in the Industrial Home two months. Looked bright and capable.

No. 46.

Born in Trenton, N. J. Irish parents. Twenty-two years old. Single. Had no trade. Had been out of work three months. In the Industrial Home three weeks. Expected money from home shortly. Never worked in the country. Said he drank a little. His appearance was very good.

No. 47.

Born in Stanwich, Conn. American parents. Twenty-six years old. Single. Had people who were poor. Had no trade. Was brought up on a farm. Came to New York one year ago after a trip through the West. Expected to go back to the country as soon as the weather got warmer. Had been in the Industrial Home ten days. Looked stupid but otherwise capable.

No. 48.

Born in Vermont. American parents. Forty-five years old. Single. Was a tool-maker by trade. Did not belong to the union. Had been out of work three months. Had been in the Industrial Home one month. Said the Army were good people. Appearance was good but somewhat dissipated. Never worked in the country.

No. 49.

Born in Seattle, Washington. Swedish parents. Twenty-eight years old. Single. Had no trade. Out of work two months. In the Industrial Home three weeks. Did not drink. Appearance was good. Never worked in the country.

No. 50.

Born in Ireland. Forty years old. Married. Separated from his wife. In this country fifteen years. Had no trade. Out of work all winter. The Army and the missions had helped him several times. Never worked in the country. Looked shiftless and dissipated.

No. 51.

Born in Scotland. Fifty years old. Single. Had no trade. Had wandered round a lot. Out of work five months. The Scotch Aid Society helped him a good deal this winter. Said he liked to drink. Never worked in the country. Looked like a tramp.

No. 52.

Born in Cleveland, O. American parents. Twenty-eight years old. Married. His wife was living in Cleveland. He left her because of a quarrel. Tool-maker by trade. Did not belong to the Union. Out of work four months. In the Industrial Home one week. Never worked in the country. Looked efficient and capable.

No. 53.

Born in Brooklyn. Irish parents. Fifty years old. Evidently married. Did not wish to talk about it. Had no trade. Out of work all winter. Had received help from the missions and the Army. Drank heavily. Appearance very poor. Never worked in the country.

No. 54.

Born in Boston, Mass. English parents. Twenty-five years old. Single. Had people in Boston, who did not help him. Had no trade. Out of work three months. In the Industrial Home two days. Said he drank sometimes. Never worked in the country. His appearance was very good.

No. 55.

Born in South America. German parents. Twenty years old. Single. Had no trade. Came from South America by working on a boat. Left it two months ago in New York, and had done nothing since. In the Industrial Home three weeks. Never worked in the country. Expected to go back on the boat shortly. Looked like a runaway boy and was bright and attractive.

No. 56.

Born in Long Island. American parents. Fifty years old. Single. Had no trade. Out of work all winter. Had rheumatism and could not do much work. The Army had helped him a good deal, but he expected to go to the hospital. Never worked in the country.

No. 57.

Born in Italy. Thirty years old. Single. Had people in Italy, who were poor. In this country twelve years. Had no trade. Out of work all winter. In the Industrial Home seven days. Said that this was the first time he had ever been out of money. Worked in the country somewhat in Italy. Looked stupid and inefficient.

No. 58.

Born in Cuba. Father American, mother Cuban. Twenty-eight years old. Single. Had people living in Panama who did not help him. Had no trade. He travelled a good deal. Came from the West two weeks ago. Got out of money, and had been in the Industrial Home one week. Looked like a promising case.

No. 59.

Born in Pittsfield, Mass. Irish parents. Fifty-five years old. Single. Had no trade, but followed the water somewhat. Had been out of work five months. In the Industrial Home two weeks. Never worked in the country. His face showed a very hard life. He was gray-haired and feeble.

No. 60.

Born in Scranton, Penna. American parents. Twenty-two years old. Single. His people were living in Scranton, but he was ashamed to write to them. Had no trade. Out of work eight weeks. In the Industrial Home one week. Never worked in the country. Looked very wild, but otherwise capable.

No. 61.

Born in New York. German parents. Thirty years old. Single. Two sisters lived in New York, but did not help him because he drank too much. Had no trade. Had had no steady work all winter. Looked dissipated. Never worked in the country.

No. 62.

Born in Ireland. Fifty years old. Married. Wife dead. No children. Had no trade. Out of work three months. Had been in the Industrial Home one month. Never worked in the country. Looked like a hard drinker.

No. 63.

Born in Chicago. American parents. Twenty-four years old. Single. People in Chicago helped him sometimes. Had no trade. Had been working in the Industrial Home in the kitchen all winter at $1.00 per week. The Army had fitted him up, and he looked very respectable.

No. 64.

Born in Germany. About forty years old. Single. No people living. Followed the water. Out of work two months. In the Industrial Home three weeks. The Army gave him clothes. He looked like a hard drinker, but otherwise capable. Never worked in the country.

No. 65.

Born in Cambridge, Mass. Irish parents. Forty-eight years old. Single. Had no trade. Had travelled all over the country. Had been out of work four months, and had been in the Industrial Home two days. Never worked in the country. Looked like a hard drinker.

No. 66.

Born in Lynn, Mass. American parents. About fifty years old. Single. Had no trade. Out of work all winter. Had travelled widely and beaten his way on freight trains. In the Industrial Home three times this winter. Never worked in the country. Looked shiftless.

No. 67.

Born in New York. Irish parents. Twenty-eight years old. Single. Quarrelled with his people. A rigger by trade. Did not belong to the Union. Out of work six weeks. In the Industrial Home ten days. Said he drank a little. Looked capable. Never worked in the country.

No. 68.

Born in Germany. About thirty years old. Single. People in Germany did not help him. Waiter by trade. In the Industrial Home two weeks. Had no steady work all Winter. Never worked in the country. Expected a position in a few days. Looked stupid, but otherwise capable.

No. 69.

Born in Philadelphia. Hungarian parents. Thirty-five years old. Single. People dead. Had no trade. Out of work all winter. Different charitable organizations had helped him. Had been in the Industrial Home one week. Did not like to work. Worked in the country a little. Looked shiftless.

No. 70.

Born in Jersey City. Irish parents. Fifty-five years old. Married. Wife dead. Had no trade. Had travelled a good deal. Out of work all winter. Had been in the Industrial Home six weeks. The Army fitted him out with clothing. He said he was not going to drink any more, and looked intelligent, but was getting old. Never worked in the country.

No. 71.

Born in Germany. Twenty-six years old. Single. In this country six years. Had people in Germany, and he expected help from them. Machinist by trade. Did not belong to the Union. Out of work four months. In the Industrial Home two days. Looked like a wild youth. Never worked in the country.

No. 72.

Born in Ireland. Forty-five years old. Single. Had no trade. Out of work all winter. Drank heavily. Worked in the country two years. Had wandered all over the States. Looked like a vagrant.

No. 73.

Born in New York. American parents. Twenty-eight years old. Single. Had no trade. Out of work all winter. In the Industrial Home four days. Army gave him clothes. The missions had helped him. Never worked in the country. Looked capable.

No. 74.

Born in Scotland. Forty-one years old. Single. Had no trade. Out of work four months. In the Industrial Home three days. Admitted that he drank heavily. Never worked in the country. Looked like a tramp.

No. 75.

Born in Chicago. American parents. Twenty-two years old. Single. People in Chicago were poor. Left home two months ago and came to New York. Spent all his money. The Army took him in, and for six weeks he had been in the Home. He wrote home. Expected to get work shortly. Looked bright and respectable.

No. 76.

Born in Boston, Mass. Irish parents. Twenty-four years old. Single. Had no trade. Had wandered a good deal. Never worked in the country. Had been in the Industrial Home one week. Did not like to work. Looked like a tramp.

No. 77.

Born in Germany. Forty years old. Married. Wife lived in Germany with two children. Had been in this country four years and expected his wife next summer. Plumber by trade. Did not belong to the Union. Out of work two months. In the Industrial Home one week, after a very hard struggle around the streets. Said he drank a little. Appearance was very good.

No. 78.

Born in Washington, D. C. Forty-five years old. Single. Had no people. Had no trade. Belonged to the United States Army six years. Out of work all winter. In the Industrial Home three weeks. Worked in the country a good deal. Looked shiftless.

No. 79.

Born in Ireland. Thirty-five years old. Single. Hod carrier by trade. Belonged to the Union. Out of work five months. In the Industrial Home four days. Looked capable and efficient. Never worked in the country.

No. 80.

Born in Germany. Fifty-two years old. Married. Wife dead. Followed the water most of the time. Out of work all winter. In the Industrial Home three days. Appearance very poor. Never worked in the country.

No. 81.

Born in New York. Twenty-eight years old. Single. People lived in New York, but did not help him. Out of work all winter. Had no trade. Had been in the Industrial Home one month. Looked like a dissipated character. Never worked in the country.

No. 82.

Born in Boston, Mass. Swedish parents. Thirty years old. Single. Iron worker by trade. Did not belong to the Union. Had been out of work five months. Had been in the

Industrial Home five weeks. Never worked in the country. He drank a good deal, but looked capable.

No. 83.

Born in England. Eighteen years old. Single. In this country two years. Had no trade. Out of work one month. Had been in the Industrial Home three weeks. Had secured a position on a ship going to England, starting in three days. Looked like a straight-forward boy.

No. 84.

Born in Albany, N. Y. American parents. Twenty-four years old. Single. Had no trade. Joined the navy two years ago. Deserted, was captured and spent one year in jail. Had been out three months and had not worked since. Had been in the Industrial Home one month. Appearance was good. Never worked in the country.

No. 85.

Born in Ireland. Fifty years old. Single. Had no trade. Had wandered all around the world. Out of work all winter. In the Industrial Home two or three times. Said he worked one year on a farm. He was crippled and looked feeble.

No. 86.

Born in Germany. Twenty-five years old. Single. People in Germany, but he did not write home. Had no trade. In this country five years. Out of work two months. Never worked in the country. Had been in the Industrial Home one day. Seemed to lack ambition.

No. 87.

Born in Denver, Colo. Irish parents. Fifty-five years old. Married. Separated from his wife five years ago. Painter by trade. Did not belong to the Union. Out of work all winter. In the Industrial Home three weeks. Appearance was very poor. Never worked in the country.

No. 88.

Born in Sweden. Twenty-two years old. Single. People at home sent him money sometimes. He said he had also sent money home. Had no trade. Out of work three months. In the Industrial Home four days. Used to work in the country in Sweden. In this country three years. Looked capable.

No. 89.

Born in Dublin, Ireland. Thirty-one years old. Single. In this country two years. Had no trade. Out of work ten weeks. In the Industrial Home three weeks. Worked in the country for a few months. Appearance was very good.

No. 90.

Born in New York. American parents. Twenty-five years old. Single. Had people in New York, but had nothing to do with them. He wandered a lot. Had no trade. Never worked in the country. Out of work all winter. The Army and missions had helped him. In the Industrial Home three days. Looked like a vagrant.

No. 91.

Born in Germany. Forty years old. Single. Had no people. Followed the water most of the time. Out of work seven months. Was in the German Hospital three months with hip disease. He was still crippled and could not work well. Had been in the Industrial Home three weeks. Looked very feeble. Never worked in the country.

No. 92.

Born in Washington, D. C. American parents. Twenty-six years old. Single. Was in the navy five years. Had no trade. Out of work all winter. In the Industrial Home three days. Never worked in the country. Acted very queerly and evidently had weak mind.

No. 93.

Born in New York. American parents. Thirty years old. Single. Carpenter by trade. Out of work four months. In the Industrial Home six weeks. The Army gave him clothing. Never worked in the country. Used to drink heavily. Looked capable.

No. 94.

Born in England. Twenty-four years old. Single. Had people in England, and he wrote home sometimes. Had no trade. Out of work three months. In the Industrial Home five weeks. Worked in the country one summer. Had been in this country three years. Did not drink. Looked very intelligent and capable.

No. 95.

Born in Providence, R. I. Irish parents. Forty-five years old. Single. Had no trade. Had beaten his way all through the country. Never worked in the country. The Army had helped him a good deal. Had been in the Home three months and said he had not taken a drink during that time. He looked bright and responsible, but showed the signs of a hard life.

No. 96.

Born in Ireland. Thirty years old. Single. People lived in Ireland. In this country four years. Never wrote home. Had no trade. Worked in the country one year. In the Industrial Home two weeks. Appearance was good but dissipated.

No. 97.

Born in Trenton, N. J. American parents. Twenty-five years old. Single. Followed the water a good deal. Out of work all winter. Had been in the Industrial Home eight weeks. Never worked in the country. Looked capable.

No. 98.

Born in Brooklyn. American parents. Twenty-six years old. Single. Had no trade. Out of work all winter. In the Industrial Home two weeks. Army gave him clothing. He looked intelligent and capable. Never worked in the country.

No. 99.

Born in Germany. Forty-five years old. People lived in Germany, but he did not write home. Had no trade. Out of work all winter. He travelled round a good deal and drank heavily. Had worked a good deal in the country. Had been in the Industrial Home four months, and said he was going to reform. Looked like a hopeful case.

No. 100.

Born in Portland, Oregon. American parents. Twenty-six years old. Single. Had no trade. Had travelled a good deal. Out of work all winter. In the Industrial Home three months. Expected money from home soon, and expected to go West. Said he had worked on a farm a good deal. Looked stupid but otherwise capable.

No. 101.

Born in Vermont. American parents. Thirty years old. Single. Carpenter by trade. Belonged to the Union. Out of work all winter. In the Industrial Home one week. Never worked in the country. The missions had helped him a good deal this winter. Looked capable.

No. 102.

Born in Boston, Mass. Irish parents. Fifty-two years old. Single. People all dead. Had no trade. Out of work four months. In the Industrial Home three weeks. Said he had ruined his life through drink. Was in the hospital two months this winter. He never worked in the country. He was crippled and could not work much.

No. 103.

Born in Chicago. American parents. Twenty-five years old. Single. Had people in Chicago, but ran away four years ago. Had no trade. Out of work three months. In the Industrial Home two months. Never worked in the country. Looked like a hopeful case.

No. 104.

Born in Cincinnati, O. American parents. Thirty-five years old. Single. Had no trade. Had wandered a good deal. Never worked in the country. In the Industrial Home two weeks. Appearance was good but dissipated.

No. 105.

Born in New York. Irish parents. Twenty-five years old. Single. Had people in New York, but they were unable to help him. Had no trade. Out of work all winter. Had been in the Industrial Home five weeks. Never worked in the country. Said he drank a little. Appearance was very good.

No. 106.

Born in Chicago. American parents. Twenty-five years old. Single. Had no trade. Out of work all winter. In the Industrial Home three months. Never worked in the country. The Army had helped him to become respectable, he said. Looked capable.

No. 107.

Born in Ireland. Forty-eight years old. Single. People dead. Had no trade. Out of work two months. Had wandered a lot. In the Industrial Home three weeks. Had worked in the country somewhat. Looked dissipated.

No. 108.

Born in St. Louis, Mo. American parents. Twenty-eight years old. Single. Had no trade. Out of work three months. The Army gave him clothes and he had been in the Industrial Home two months. Never worked in the country. Looked inefficient.

No. 109.

Born in Sweden. Forty years old. Single. Had people in Sweden. Had no trade. Out of work all winter. Had been in Industrial Home three months. Army gave him clothing. Did not drink. Looked capable and efficient. Never worked in the country.

Some Facts Brought Out in the 109 Industrial Examples. [36]

Nationality. No. Percentage.

American parentage 41 .376

Irish parentage 30 .276

German parentage 18 .165

English and Scotch parentage 9 .083

Italian parentage 3 .027

Swedish parentage 3 .027

Other countries, parentage 5 .046

Married 17 .156

Single 92 .844

Worked a little in country 16 .146

Worked considerably in country 7 .064

Men with regular trades 31 .289

Union men 6 .055

Men who looked efficient 38 .349

Men who looked semi-efficient 21 .193

Men who looked inefficient 50 .458

Ages.

15-20 2 .018

20-30 55 .504

30-40 23 .212

40-50 20 .183

50-60 8 .074

60-70 1 .009

Length of time out of work.

Less than 1 month 8 .073

More than 1 month 17 .156

More than 2 months 16 .146

More than 3 months. [37] 68 .625

FOOTNOTES:

[14] "Prospectus of the Salvation Army Industrial Homes Company."

[15] "The Poor and the Land," p. 130.

[16] Haggard places it at 500 in 1905; at the time of my visit, May, 1906, it was about 300.

[17] "Hadleigh," p. 52.

[18] "The Poor and the Land," p. 127.

[19] "The S. A. and the Public," pp. 113-114.

[20] Ibid., p. 114.

[21] Ibid., p. 105.

[22] "Hadleigh," p. 56.

[23] Apparently no definite data are obtainable regarding these men since the time of treatment.

[24] Introduction, p. 10.

[25] For instance, the president, vice-president and secretary and treasurer are all Army officers of high standing.

[26] The following extract is taken from the Salvation Army Social Gazette of February 5, 1908: "Whether the Officer of the Salvation Army takes charge of the industrial

home to manage it in the interests of the concern, or whether he takes charge of the corps, the one great purpose of his whole life is to proclaim salvation to all with whom he comes in contact."

[27] See p. 36.

[28] We think that this would probably be done, even though the presence of the home in the particular locality was a great boon to the poor, and although this would be contrary to the principles of the organization, so strong is the idea which the company has of financial success. This further strengthens the idea that the movement is drifting from its original purpose of uplifting the down-fallen humanity to the purpose of perpetuating and extending itself as an economic enterprise.

[29] See "The S. A. and the Public," pp. 121 to 130.

[30] A typical industry instanced to support this objection was the manufacture of fire wood. See "The S. A. and the Public," p. 124.

[31] The criticism here of course would be that, to the extent that the army applies donations from the public to this industrial work, to that extent it has an advantage over another business enterprise and differs from it just to that extent in which it secures capital on which it need pay no interest or return. To what extent this is done, we have been unable to ascertain, but the Army is paying interest to investors who furnish money to carry on this work. This point is dealt with somewhat in the next paragraph.

[32] See "The S. A. and the Public," pp. 122 to 127. Also "The Social Relief Work of the S. A.," pp. 11 and 12.

[33] Several leading officers have stated that they never undersell paper or rags, the largest part of their business, and that the only underselling done by them is in the retail store and that this is slight. They justify themselves by the fact that the regular second-hand men are tricksters and will rob the poor of their money, in most cases carrying on a pawn shop, which the Army never does.

[34] See Seager, "Introduction to Economics," p. 234.

[35] See "Principles of Relief," p. 35.

[36] To show the difference in the grade of the men at the Industrial Homes and those at the Hotels, I have given separate tables for each. The combined tables showing certain characteristics of the class of men in general with which the Army deals will be found at the end of Chapter IV.

[37] This number includes all the inefficient men and the men who are steadily working in the Industrial Home.

CHAPTER II.

The Salvation Army Hotels and Lodging Houses.

In a study of environment and its effects on the lowest classes of our great cities, the cheap lodging house affords a favorable field. Here we have crowding, unsanitary conditions, immoral atmosphere, and all the attendant evils. A good description of such lodging houses in New York City has been given by Jacob Riis, in the following words:

"In the caravansaries that line Chatham Street and the Bowery, harboring nightly a population as large as that of many a thriving town, a home-made article of tramp and thief is turned out that is attracting the increasing attention of the police, and offers a field for the missionary's labors, besides which most others seem of slight consequence" [38].

The cheap lodging houses of London and other great cities are similar in their environment and effects. This field was early entered by the Army. It was necessary that a very low rate of cost for the individual concerned be maintained because of competition with the lodging houses already existing, and because of the size of the prospective lodger's purse. The first experiments were tried in London. There, at first, the primary aim was to aid the needy and destitute, but later the Army entered into a competition with the existing lodging houses and paid more attention to the element of environment. It was soon definitely proved that such a work could be carried on to advantage, that shelter amid beneficial surroundings, could be provided to those almost destitute, and that the work could be self-supporting. Since then this work has extended to nearly all the larger cities of Europe and America, but it is of greatest extent in England and the United States. Along with this growth there has been differentiation. The hotels have been graded to suit the requirements of the different classes to which they appeal: the almost destitute class, and those who have steady employment. Hence, besides treating of conditions common to both, we shall describe special features of two grades of both men's and women's hotels. [39]

The location for a men's hotel must be determined partly by its propinquity to the class of men which it is seeking to attract and partly for facilities for ventilation, cleanliness and general sanitary conditions. These last features are of the greatest importance in this work. Led by the real need of the case, and working with regard to its reputation, the Army has, in this respect, shown a great advance over the general cheap lodging houses. Still, there is room for improvement in the Army hotels. [40] One great difficulty lies in the lodgers, many of whom are so habituated to uncleanliness in general, that it is with great reluctance on their part that they are induced to cleanliness. Especially in the lower class hotels is this true where the rough, brutal element finds its way. Another difficulty lies in the fact that the Army frequently takes old buildings and turns them into hotels, when they are not suitable for the purpose. A favorable tendency to overcome this, however, lies in the Army's desire to put up new buildings fitted for hotels, and this is being done in many cities.

In both the higher and the lower class men's hotels, the general plan is to have two or three grades of sleeping apartments. The first grade is in the form of dormitories, where each dormitory will contain from ten to fifty beds in the smaller hotels, and from fifty to one hundred and even two hundred beds in the larger. [41] For a bed in one of these dormitories, 10c and 15c per night is charged in the United States, and in England 2d up. This includes the use of a locker beside the bed, with sometimes a nightgown, and sometimes a bath. The second grade of lodging is in individual rooms, partitioned off, but inside rooms, for which the charge is 15c in the United States, and 4d to 6d in England. Then finally we have the third grade of lodging, which consists of individual rooms which have outside windows, and for which the price varies from 20c to 50c per night according to situation and furnishing. [42] Sometimes the three grades of lodging are found on the same floor, a part of the floor being dormitory, and a part partitioned off into rooms, the partitions running up to a height of eight or nine feet. This method of partitioning off the rooms is almost universal. It is cheap and to some extent sanitary, since by means of windows at either end of the building a continual current of air can be maintained all over the floor. In most of the higher class hotels one floor is given up to dormitories and another to individual rooms, while the majority of lower class hotels consist entirely of dormitories. Hotels are of all sizes, and run from one floor up to eight or ten.

The beds found in the Army hotels are iron, with mattresses usually covered with American cloth or some form of leather, but sometimes with strong canvas. [43] Each bed is provided with pillow, sheets, a coverlid, and sometimes an additional counterpane. The individual rooms, in addition to having better beds, contain a looking glass, a chair, a small table, and other furnishings according to the price of the room. In most cases washing facilities are only found in the lavatory, common to the whole floor.

Comparative cleanliness is enforced at all grades of hotels. Baths are sometimes made compulsory, though often this rule cannot be rigidly enforced. Usually each floor is provided with bath tubs and shower baths. Nearly every hotel has a fumigating room, an air tight apartment filled with racks, upon which clothing is hung. If a man's appearance or clothing looks suspicious in any way, his clothes are placed in a sack with a number corresponding to the number of his bed or room, and hung in the fumigating room over night. Early the next morning his clothes will be returned to him. The dormitories and rooms themselves, every few days, receive a fumigating and cleaning. Thus, except in very rare cases, no fault can be found with the cleanliness of the Army hotels. We hardly ever visited any of them without coming into contact with the scent of fumigation, or finding some individual working with mop and broom.

The above description, except where stated differently, fits both classes of men's hotels. The higher class, intended for transients of the better class of poor and for workmen with steady employment, has some distinctive features. In addition to better equipment along the line of furnishings, lavatories, etc., this class of hotels necessarily has a better social environment than the other. For instance, there are many lower class hotels where the reading room is dark, poorly furnished, without attractive reading matter, and where it serves as smoking room as well as reading room. While this might be improved, yet so low are the occupants that such improvement would not be appreciated. But when we come to the higher grade hotels, we find a difference. Take, for example, the Army Hotel in the city of Cleveland, O., on the corner of Eagle and Erie Streets. This corner building was built by the Army to answer its purpose, at a cost of $100,000.00. There are no dormitories in the building. The three upper floors are given over to the hotel, which comprises 130 rooms, each room being steam heated and electric lighted, and each floor being reached by elevators. Bathing facilities and sanitary arrangements are first class. A comfortable reading room and lounging room is provided for general use, where there are popular magazines, daily papers and writing conveniences. As another example, about the highest grade Army institution of this class is found in Boston, and is called "The People's Palace." It is a large, five-story, corner building, built by the Army for the purpose. In this institution the social environment is especially emphasized. There is a reading room, a smoking room, one or more social parlors, a gymnasium with a swimming tank, and an auditorium with a seating capacity of 600. The whole building, with its 287 single rooms, besides the above advantages, is equipped with steam heat, electric service and other modern conveniences. A special fee of 25c is charged for the use of the gymnasium and swimming tank, but the other advantages are free to lodgers. In this way, it is seen that the higher class hotels have more opportunity for a good social environment and for social work. We think that the addition of certain features, such as men's clubs, smokers, popular lectures, etc., would be of great advantage to this class of institutions. To overcome the difficulty of a transient population, however, would require considerable ingenuity. [44]

Along the line of religious environment we find the hotels differ a great deal. In London there seems to be a strong influence of this kind, most of the hotels of both classes holding gospel meetings frequently. For instance, at the Quaker Street Elevator Home, which is partly a hotel and partly an industrial home, meetings are held nearly every night with good attendance, and at the Burne Street Hotel well attended meetings are held every night except Wednesdays and Saturdays, these nights being given over to the men for washing their clothes. But in the United States we find, as a rule, that the Salvation Army hotels are run with very little religious influence. In a few cases, meetings are held regularly, but more often no provision is made for them. Meetings are generally in progress somewhere in the neighborhood at the regular Army corps, and the men are left to attend these meetings if they wish. Generally they are willing to take advantage of the hotel, but do not care for the sentimental form of religion preached by the Army. Hence, in most of the hotels, we find the religious influence limited to the texts on the walls, and to the attitude of the employees, who are not always Salvationists or converted men.

Some hotels of both classes are fitted with a kitchen and lunch counter. This is nearly always the case in London, where the hotels have a counter, over which the food is sold, and then taken to a seat by the purchaser. In several cases the counter is divided so that it opens into different rooms, and there are two grades of prices, the lower price being paid for food somewhat damaged and stale. [45]

We need not dwell long on the subject of the women's hotels, as that does not form an important part of the Army's work. The women's hotels, even more than the men's, have tended to fall into two classes. There is a great difference between the hotel for women who are almost destitute, and the hotel for respectable working girls, who have positions as clerks and stenographers, and who happen to have no home of their own. A typical hotel of the former class is situated near the Dearborn Street Railway Depot in Chicago. It consists of three floors, and has accommodation for fifty girls or women. The woman officer in charge lives here herself, and seeks to have an environment as homelike as possible. She states, however, that occasionally the women come in noisily and are troublesome. There is a great difference between one woman and another, and she wishes she had one floor with better accommodation than the rest for the better element among them. The price paid per bed at this hotel is 10 cents. A good example of this class of hotel in England, is the one situated on Hanbury Street, Whitechapel, London, where there are three floors, two upper floors given over to dormitories containing 276 beds in all, and the ground floor containing a dining room, kitchen, small hall, and office. Here, women are turned away quite often because of lack of room. 2d. is charged for a bed, and for food a scale of prices, such as tea, ½d.—soup, ½d.—bread, ½d.—etc. There are nine officers working here, and nine other workers, six of the latter receiving 3s. per week, and three receiving 1s. per week.

With the higher class hotels for women, the Army has not had much success. This is easily understood, as the respectable girl does not like to be connected with a hotel run by an organization which is prominent for its slum and rescue work. These hotels charge a higher rate for rooms and are situated in a good quarter of the city. [46] They are frequented by shop girls, bookkeepers, clerks and stenographers. Apparently, no great religious pressure is brought to bear on the girls and women, but this would probably depend on the officer in charge.

The growth of the Hotel Department of the Army's work, like that of the Industrial Department, has, of recent years, been great. Soon after the publication in 1890 of General Booth's book, "Darkest England," the hotel work was started in England, and its progress has been rapid. In the

United States at first the work did not make much headway. When Commander Booth-Tucker came to take charge in 1896, there were three small men's hotels situated in the cities of Buffalo, San Francisco, and Seattle. At the present time, nearly every large city in England and the United States has one or more of these hotels, the latter country having 71 men's hotels and 4 women's hotels, with a total accommodation of 8,688. The tendency now is toward fewer of the lower class hotels, and more of the higher class; in other words, toward fewer hotels where beds can be had for 10c and 15c, and more where they will cost 20c and 25c. The Army gives as its reason for this the fact that the cheaper hotel cannot be maintained in a wholesome manner and be self-supporting. [47] Similar to the Industrial Department in its management, the Hotel Department has its divisions, its graded officers with their various responsibilities, and its head officer in charge at the national headquarters. In the United States, however, unlike the Industrial Department, the Hotel Department has no separate financial company, in the form of a corporation, behind it. In some instances, deserving men are given bed tickets and meal tickets free, by officers detailed for the purpose, and, to that extent the hotels are a charity. This is done with due discretion and does not make an appreciable difference. The amount of charity indulged in by the Army in this way is, however, probably responsible for the fact that in 1907, there was a loss to the Army in this department of $4,500.00, not a very large amount, considering the number of hotels concerned.

Coming to the value of the Army hotels from the point of view of the social economist, care must be taken to discriminate between their commercial and their philanthropic aspects. The public has a mistaken idea of the work carried on by this branch of the Army. Many people have an idea that thousands of homeless, starving men and women are nightly taken care of in these Army hotels. Putting aside the question whether such would be good relief policy or not, the statement itself is not true. In a majority of cases the man or woman in order to gain admittance must have the price, and in many instances, that price will also admit them to the regular cheap lodging house outside of the Army. We are not finding fault with the system of charging, since from the point of view of true relief, provided that bona-fide, destitute cases are not left without help, the price should be required, as it would be a great evil to throw open the hotels to the crowds of regular beggars and social parasites who constantly throng any institution supposed to be charitable; but since the Army hotel movement claims to be a self-supporting business, it is not to be regarded as different from any other lodging business, except in those points in which it excels the other. With this caution we believe that we still can distinguish two lines along which credit is to be given the Army. The first is the environment which the Army has created for its guests. It is not necessary here to show what a great factor environment is in this case, but simply to emphasize its importance. From our description of the Army hotel, it is seen that, with certain exceptions, the Army maintains cleanliness, cheerfulness, and a homelike atmosphere around its lodging houses. [48] In this important respect then, the Army hotel is to be commended. Secondly, the Army has indirectly, by its competition with the ordinary cheap lodging houses, led them to adopt improvement for purely commercial reasons. If a man has only ten cents, he is going to invest that ten cents to the best advantage, and the old time lodging houses have found it necessary to improve their conditions in order to meet the competition of the Army. For this too, credit is to be given the latter. In addition the competition reacts on the Army and tends to make it keep up its own standard.

In order more clearly to discuss the advantages and disadvantages of cheap lodging houses, whether Army hotels or not, it would be well here to consider objections to their existence. Three objections have been raised to all cheap lodging houses in general.

1. That they herd together a low class of vagrants and vicious characters.

2. That their cheapness lowers the standard of living.

3. That they encourage the youth of the country to come to the city and live in comparative idleness. [49]

No one who has looked into the matter has any doubt about the accuracy of the first objection. One glance at the faces of a group of men in the smoking room of any such hotel reveals many of the low, bestial, criminal type; many victims of dissipation and many who have acquired a dislike for work of any sort. This harboring of the vicious element is also true of the Army hotels of the lower class, but it is in company with this element that we find the men for whom more or less can be done. [50]

The second objection must be considered more carefully. To repeat the definition of the standard of living which was discussed in connection with the Industrial Department, it is the scale or measure of comfort and satisfaction, which a person or community of persons, regards as indispensable to happiness. Now the question is whether these cheap lodging houses lower this standard; whether their existence results in a tendency to live with less effort and less ambition, and thus renders men and women less productive and less proficient. This question must be separated into a question regarding the community as a whole, and a question regarding the individual. As regards the standard of living of any single community, the answer would be that the standard is not appreciably lowered by this hotel system, since the occupants are mostly single men wandering around, and the standard of living of the community is more concerned with the maintenance of homes in its midst, than of transients. This, however, brings in the further question as to whether the cheap living made possible by the lodging houses leads to the breaking up of homes, since if it does so, it would bear decidedly on the standard of living. We would answer this second question in the negative, because life in the cheap hotel is not such a desirable thing as to lead to the breaking up of homes. A man has already left home and is already reduced in circumstances, before the fact of such cheap living as the hotels and cheap restaurants of the Bowery in New York, or of Whitechapel in London, ever comes to him as an advantage. But, on the other hand, when it comes to the individual concerned, we think that the standard is lowered and that in many cases the objection holds good. For instance, take a man with a regular trade, say bricklaying or carpentering. He is thrown out of work and gradually drifts down to the cheap hotel. For months, possibly, he strives in vain to get work at his trade. He exists, however, by means of odd jobs picked up at random; he becomes shiftless; the life which consists of so much "hanging around" and loafing, decreases his efficiency, and, in this way, his standard is lowered. At the same time his character is affected, and even if no worse development takes place, he loses ambition, and that lowers his standard. Hence, in conclusion, we would say that the objection that the hotel movement of the Army leads to a lowering of a standard of living has no place as regards the community, but is sustained as regards individuals.

The third objection that the country youth are induced by this cheap living to leave for the city is not a strong one and needs but short notice. Some of the most successful men of our cities come from the country, but very few of the lower and pauper classes. This has been shown by the investigations of Mr. Fox in England, and by our own investigations in the United States. [51]

The consideration of these objections leads us to a closer examination of the class of men frequenting the hotels of the Army. The men's work being so much larger, let us look at the occupants of the men's hotels. Here we must separate the comparatively few hotels of the higher class, which, charging higher prices and harboring the working man, have a different environment from the others. In these, the higher class, we see a competition with the ordinary boarding and lodging houses which single men frequent, a competition which, owing to the more healthful social environment of the Army hotel, is to be welcomed and approved of as a preventive of vice and degradation. The latter is often the result of crowded, uncleanly, workingmen's lodgings, which drive their occupants to the saloon. But the majority of the Army hotels are filled with the lowest class of men, out of any steady employment. This class is composed for the most part and under present conditions, of men who are almost helpless cases. [52] Conditions can be conceived which would result in the betterment of a certain percentage of these, but a large number would always be hopeless. Many have been given their chances and have thrown them away; some have had no chances, and some could not use them if they had. Many are physical and moral wrecks. In their faces you see no ambition. They simply exist as do animals. For such, except in unusual cases, there is no remedy. Do all you can for them, and they will slide back again; give them work, and if they are willing to take it at all, they soon lose their positions. Some belong to the pseudo-social class and are mere parasites feeding on society. Others are anti-social, bitter and criminal. [53]

These men are not those with which the Army is successful, in its industrial institutions, although many of them have been tried. They secure their ten cents or fifteen cents for a bed in a cheap hotel by any means which comes along. They form a class, which especially in the older countries of Europe and increasingly in the new world, presents a problem that is the great puzzle of the statesman and the social economist alike.

The present tendency of the Army already mentioned to have fewer of the lower class, cheap hotels and more of the higher class brings up some important considerations. There are three points which come up for particular notice here. First, as has already been stated, the present tendency of the Army is to have fewer of the lower class or cheap hotels and more of the higher class. One reason for this is that, although the Army's competition has in many instances forced the ordinary cheap hotels to better their equipment, still, in the long run, the Army cannot successfully compete with the ordinary low class hotel and maintain an equally good or better environment, without having its hotel work subsidized by the public. The men whom we have just described do not appreciate better surroundings sufficiently to pay fifteen cents for a bed at the Army hotel, when they can get one for ten cents at another place around the corner. Secondly, as the Army extends its work, there is the ever present tendency of any organization to become an end in itself. Hence the Army tends to forsake its field of the lower class for the field of the working class for financial reasons. If it can carry on a hotel which appeals to a higher class of working men who are willing to pay $1.50 upwards per week for a separated room such as has been described, they may do better financially than with a dormitory whose beds are held at ten cents. This second point of consideration leads us to a third, and that is, what is to become of this lower class of vagrants and unemployables. This discussion hardly comes in the scope of this book, but we might suggest in passing that the cheap, lower class of hotels with which the Army has entered into competition should not be allowed to continue as at present. In case of the failure to provide competition, the city itself should provide a successful competition under good environment, or should take measures for the segregation of the vicious elements of the population from the merely weak, aged and unfortunate. [54]

On the other hand, among the occupants of these hotels a certain number are men for whom there is hope; some victims of misfortune; others degraded by dissipation and recklessness, but not entirely demoralized. With these the Army can deal successfully in its industrial homes, and some of them can regain a foothold without aid. For these men the Army hotel is certainly a boon. [55] A man who has not lost ambition and who can gather a few cents a day to sustain him, until some temporary difficulty is past is glad to take advantage of such an institution. Finally, regarding this class as a whole, something must be done with them, and it is necessary for those who find fault with their congregation in the Army hotels, to point out a better way of caring for them. As long as they exist, they will tend to congregate somewhere, and until some better solution is offered, we might as well take what is at hand, and if it is the Army hotel, hold that institution to its best efforts and its best environment.

To sum up, then, our conclusions of this part of the Army's work, we find that the hotels are commercial enterprises, with, as a rule, an environment superior to the regular cheap hotels of the same price, and that although there is an objection to the congregation of the vicious and vagrant along with the unfortunate, and although there may be a tendency to lower the standard of living of these people, individually considered, yet there is a justification for the existence of these hotels, as something must be done with this class of people, and this is the best solution offered, inasmuch as a certain percentage of this class is really aided and tided over temporary difficulty. At the same time, there remains the need of the segregation of the class concerned, with a more scientific, practical, individual treatment. Better work can be done along this line.

Examples of Salvation Army Hotel Lodgers.

A collection of 76 cases made on seventeen different evenings during the months of March and April, 1908, at two of the Salvation Army hotels, both situated on the Bowery in New York City, one being a lower class hotel and the other a combination of lower and higher class. These cases were collected at first hand by the author and a friend of the author, Mr. James Ward, both of whom mingled among the men in the disguise of working men. In this way the facts were gained without much difficulty, with the exception of information regarding the family of the man concerned. Sometimes, therefore, this latter information is lacking.

No. 1.

Born in New York City of Irish parentage. Twenty-five years old. Single. Had no home and did not know whether or not his people were living. Only trade was that of hotel porter but had done other things. Had worked a little in the country. Had had no steady work for three months. Walked the streets the previous night and had had coffee and rolls on the "bread line." Received a bed that night through charity. Did not appear dissipated but showed lack of ambition.

No. 2.

Born in Ireland. About thirty years old. Single. Did not know about his people as he did not write home. Had been in New York seven years. Worked as stableman most of the time but had been out of steady work for six weeks. Never worked in the country. Appeared dissipated and inefficient.

No. 3.

Born in Pittsburg of American parents. About forty years old. Single. Had a brother, he thought, in Pittsburg but no other relatives alive. Had no regular trade. Had travelled a good deal in the United States but never west of Chicago. Had done odd jobs in the country. Evidently a tramp. Looked stupid and incapable.

No. 4.

Born in Germany. About twenty-three years old. Single. Wrote to his people sometimes, but they were poor. Trade, a waiter. Had worked in New York for five years. Had had no steady work for over two months. Had a little money saved but that was nearly gone. Expected to go to Albany the next day to work. Never worked in the country. Appeared to be a capable, steady man.

No. 5.

Born in Scotland. Fifty-three years old. Single. People all dead except a married sister. Regular trade, a boiler-maker. In this country most of the time for thirty-five years. Had travelled all around the world. Never worked in the country. Had no steady work all winter, but obtained work for one or two days every week and thus paid his way at the hotel. Said he lived up to his salary when working steadily. Is growing old. Sometimes went on a "spree" when he had money. Looked like a hard-working, efficient man.

No. 6.

Born in Ireland. About forty years old. Had married and separated from his wife. Trade was brick-laying, but he was not a union man. Never worked in the country. Came to New York at eighteen and had been there most of the time since. Claimed to be a Mason, and said that he expected help from a friend. Had been out of work all winter but worked occasionally around saloons and nearly always had the price of a bed. Admitted drinking heavily. Looked dissipated.

No. 7.

Born in Buffalo of American parents. Twenty-eight years old. Single. Waiter by trade. Parents were dead. Had two brothers but did not know where. Had worked a little in the country but knew nothing of farming. Had worked as waiter in New York for three years. Got into a fight three weeks before and had his face disfigured. As a result lost his job. Walked the streets two nights last week. Got coffee and rolls on the "bread line." Worked in a stable yesterday and made $1.00. Appeared somewhat dissipated but intelligent.

No. 8.

Born in New York City. Father German. Mother Scotch. Thirty-two years old. Single. His father lived somewhere in New York, and he expected to get work shortly and live with him. Trade was a machinist. Had mostly worked at bicycle repairing. Had travelled a good deal but never worked on a farm. Went to Philadelphia this Winter and lost position. Worked three days in a woodyard for board and lodging. Later had himself committed to jail for one month. Came back to New York last week. Did not appear dissipated, but looked bright and efficient.

No. 9.

Born in Lawrence, Mass., of American parents. About twenty-two years old. Single. Worked since a boy in Lawrence in the woolen mills until he lost position six weeks previously. Always lived with his people. Had never been hungry or without a bed. Came to New York two weeks previously but had done nothing since. Had just money enough left to go home, where he expected to obtain work again shortly. Looked thoroughly capable and reliable.

Nos. 10 and 11.

Two brothers born in New York of Irish parentage. Aged twenty-eight and thirty-one respectively. Both single. Parents dead. Had trade of awning makers, with plenty of work in summer but none in winter. Had never worked in the country. Had been living by means of odd jobs and charity all winter. Had received help from a mission and the Salvation Army. Quite often walked the streets all night and got coffee and rolls on the "bread line." Appeared shiftless and showed lack of initiative and intelligence.

No. 12.

Born in New York City of Irish parents. Twenty-six years old. Single. Did not know where his folks were. His mother was dead. Worked sometimes as a truck driver. Had worked at farm work in New Jersey. Had travelled a good deal. Had received help from charities in different cities. Got caught once riding a freight train through Philadelphia and spent ten days in jail for the offense. Said he drank when he got the chance. Now worked around the Army Hotel and received in return his bed and one meal ticket a day. Expected to leave the city as soon as the weather got warmer. Evidently a kind of tramp with a tendency to become worse. Looked wild and unreliable.

No. 13.

Born in Watertown, N. Y., of American parents. About thirty years old. Single. Had lost track of his people.

Worked as steward on ship running to New Orleans. Was laid off three months ago. Expected to get position as steward again in the spring. Had walked the streets quite often, not being able to secure a bed. Had received help from several charities, including the Army. Looked dissipated and unreliable. Had never worked in the country.

No. 14.

Born in England. Came to this country when sixteen. People all dead. Thirty-two years old. Single. Never worked in the country. Regular trade was that of a painter but was not a Union man. Got odd jobs from time to time in paint shops. Made fifty cents the previous day. Had had no steady work for three months. Had forty dollars saved when he left his last steady job. Spent twenty dollars on a "drunk," and the rest had gone since. Appeared capable and fairly intelligent.

No. 15.

Born in Germany. Had come to this country with his people when young. His people all dead except a sister who was married and lived in Chicago. Single. About thirty-five years of age. Had no regular trade. Had worked as laborer in both country and city. Said that the city was best in Winter and the country in Summer. Expected to leave for the country as soon as the weather grew warm. Appeared lazy and inefficient. Had been aided by the Army. Evidently a tramp.

No. 16.

Born in Pittsfield, Mass., of American parents. Twenty-four years of age. Single. Ran away from home at seventeen. Did not know where his people were. Had no trade. Had worked at everything. Was in the navy for four years and afterward followed the water for several years working mostly as fireman. Never worked in the country. Had been out of steady work for six months. Secured lodging through charity but often spent the night on the streets. Said he drank when he could get it. Looked dissipated and demoralized.

No. 17.

Born in New York City of German parents. About thirty years old. Married but had left his wife. Had no regular trade. Had worked as waiter, porter and liveryman. Made fifty cents yesterday but spent forty for whiskey. Secured coffee and rolls on the "bread line." Had worked a little in the country. Appeared shiftless.

No. 18.

Born in Germany. Twenty-two years of age. Single. Wrote to his people sometimes. Always followed the water. Had sailed from different points to China and the Philippines. Drank and lost his boat. Made his way to New York where he had been out of work for two months. Wrote home for money which he expected shortly. Sold some of his clothing to get a bed. Was trying to get work on a boat. Never worked in the country. Looked wild and dissipated.

No. 19.

Born in Boston, Mass., of Irish parents. Twenty-five years of age. Single. Worked in machine shop when a boy and then joined the navy. After the navy experience he had worked both on water and on land. Had beaten his way on freight trains to different parts of the United States. Said he often got help from missions. Often slept in the parks in summer. Had been in jail several times. The last time for four months for stealing. Got out in August and had done odd jobs since. Had been several times in the Army hotel and several times in the City Lodging House. Had worked for a day or so in the country but did not know farming. Looked shiftless and demoralized.

No. 20.

Born in Binghamton, N. Y., of American parents. About thirty-five years of age. Single. Trade was lasting shoes in a shoe factory. Had worked in different cities but never in the country. Came to New York three months ago, as his factory had laid off a large number of hands. Had done odd jobs since. Walked the streets three nights the previous week and got coffee and rolls on the "bread line." Got a bed for the night this time through charity. Expected to get work in a factory when the weather became warmer. Drank occasionally but not often. Looked competent and of average intelligence.

No. 21.

Born in Ireland. Twenty-four years old. Single. Left home and had been in America one year. Worked in New York as waiter and lost his position three weeks previous to interview. Had some money saved but drank and lost it all on the Bowery. Walked the streets for one week and frequented the "bread line." Had a position, now, waiting on table during the dinner hour. Used to work on a farm in Ireland, and said that as soon as the weather got warm he would go to the country and look for work. Looked somewhat dissipated but hopeful.

No. 22.

Born in Brooklyn, N. Y. Twenty-six years old. Single. Had no trade. Had lost track of his people. Had travelled a good deal by means of freight trains and had been in several jails for vagrancy. Had never worked in the country. Said when he could get money, he spent it in drink. Secured a bed that night through an acquaintance. Looked like a confirmed tramp and vagrant.

No. 23.

Born in Hartford, Conn., of American parents. Twenty-one years old. Single. Parents dead. Had a married sister living in New Jersey, but he did not wish her to know that he was out of work. Had been working for years as a carpenter's assistant and hoped to become a full-fledged carpenter shortly. Had never worked in the country. Had been out of work for three months. Spent his money in a vain trip to Philadelphia and back looking for work. Had been doing odd jobs but had often gone hungry. Did not like to ask for charity. Expected to work as soon as the contractors began the spring building. Did not drink. Looked intelligent, bright, and was a very hopeful case. Went through the grammar school.

No. 24.

Born in Boston of Irish parents. Fifty years old. Single. Had no people living. Trade was a hardwood finisher. Never worked in the country. Got out of work two months ago. Left Boston then and came to New York. Had a little money, but it was almost gone. Was crippled but could still work. Drank some. He was gray-haired and looked older than he was.

No. 25.

Born in Ireland. About sixty years old. Had been married, but his wife was dead, and he had no known relatives. Had been a seaman a good deal but had no regular trade. He worked on a farm two months in the West. Had travelled a good deal. He worked occasionally around the docks and made just enough to maintain himself. When he had money, he spent it rashly. Looked like a hard drinker.

No. 26.

Born in Boston of American parents. Fifty-seven years old. Single. Had no people. His trade was ship's cook. He had never worked in the country. Said that he was too old to get a position. He secured a bed that night through the kindness of a friend, also out of work. Had wandered around a great deal. He did not look dissipated but he was gray-haired and very feeble.

No. 27.

Born in Philadelphia of German parents. About forty years old. Single. Trade was that of a sign-painter. Said he had worked mostly in Philadelphia and New York, and that he could get plenty of work, but kept losing his positions through drink. Had never worked in the country. Said he had people in Philadelphia but he did not write to them. Looked dissipated.

No. 28.

Born near Lynn, Mass., of American parents. Twenty years old. Single. Had no trade, but worked as dish-washer or at anything he could get. Said that he could run an engine and had been working on a boat in New York harbor but had to leave three weeks ago, on account of sickness. Was trying to get into a hospital. Money nearly gone. Was born and brought up on a farm but ran away nearly three years ago and did not want to go back, though his father and mother were living. Said he spent his money freely when he had it. He did not look dissipated but appeared to be a consumptive.

No. 29.

Born in New York City of Irish parents. About thirty-five years old. Single. Had no trade but had worked for years as driver on a horse-car. Got out of work four months ago and had no prospect of any. Got a small job cleaning out a saloon the previous day. Often walked the streets all night and went to the "bread line." Did not look very dissipated but evidently had no ambition. Did not know where his people were. Never worked in the country.

No. 30.

Born in Ireland. Sixteen years old. Single. Did not write home. Had trade of a cook and had been out of work for two weeks. Then had $100.00 and lost it all "on a drunk."

Never worked in the country. Had walked the streets three nights the past week. Was going to New Jersey to look for work. Looked dissipated but otherwise capable.

No. 31.

Born in Scotland. Fifty-five years old. Married in Scotland and came with family to this country twenty-five years ago. Had no trade. Worked at anything he could get. Wife dead. Two children living, unable to help him. Had travelled widely. Obtained a steady job the previous month. Held it two weeks, then went "on a drunk." Still had enough money saved to keep him two weeks. Said that if he did not get work before then, he would leave New York. He knew a little about farm work in Scotland. Looked like a hard drinker.

No. 32.

Born in New York City of Irish parents. Sixty years old. Single. People all dead. Had no regular trade but had followed the water. Never worked in the country. Had some cousins in New York who helped him out a little. He looked dissipated and feeble.

No. 33.

Born in Philadelphia. American parents. Forty-three years old. Single. Salesman. Had been out of work all winter after losing a position through drink. Had received help from several aid societies and missions this winter. Had walked the streets a good many nights. Said he never worked in the country. Looked dissipated and unreliable.

No. 34.

Born in South Carolina. American parents. Twenty years old. Single. Did not write home. Said he ran away and his people were angry. Had no trade. Never worked in the country. Had walked the streets two nights this week. Looked intelligent but wild.

No. 35.

Born in Newark, N. J., English parents. Twenty-six years old. Single. Had no trade but worked as a janitor. Was in the navy for three years and had travelled widely. Had been out of work one month. Never worked in the country. Said he worked for a while and then "went off on a drunk." His people in Newark sent him money once in a while. Looked dissipated.

No. 36.

Born in Ireland. Thirty-eight years old. Single. When seven years old came to America with his people. Had two brothers and one sister in Schenectady, N. Y. Parents dead. His people did not aid him as he drank so much. Never worked in the country. Got an odd job now and then. Looked like a hard drinker.

No. 37.

Born in England. Thirty-six years old. Single. Came to America with his people when twelve years old. Went to Fall River, Mass., where his people lived. Ran away from home at eighteen and had followed the water since. Never worked in the country. Was paid off last Saturday. Went on a drunk on the Bowery and lost his money and his job. Walked the streets two nights, but received help from his people. Looked a little dissipated but capable.

No. 39.

Born in Yonkers, N. Y. American parents. Forty years old. Single. Father lived in Yonkers but was unable to help him. Plumber by trade. Did not belong to the Union. Was out of work for one month the past winter, but now had a job and was renting a room in the Army hotel. Never worked in the country. Looked like a hard drinker, but otherwise capable.

No. 40.

Born in New Haven, Conn. American parents. Twenty-five years old. Single. Relatives in New Haven poor. Was a telegraph operator and worked at that trade for two years, but lost position on account of bad health. Had worked on a farm quite a little, and said as soon as the weather got warmer he was going to the country. He now had a room at the Army hotel but his money was nearly gone. Looked intelligent and capable.

No. 41.

Born in New York City. American parents. Twenty-four years old. Single. Did not know where his relatives were. Had trade as truck driver, and since losing a steady job two months previously had worked at odd jobs about the docks. Spent two days at an Army Industrial Home and was now at the Army Hotel. He looked like a hard drinker. Never worked in the country.

No. 42.

Born in Scotland. Twenty-three years old. Single. Relatives lived in Scotland and sent him a little money sometimes. Had no regular trade. Had worked on the water a good deal. Came to New York two years previously, and had no steady work since. Had been nine months in the hospital from which he had been discharged two weeks. Expected to return to the hospital. Looked like a very sick man, but not dissipated.

No. 43.

Born in New York City. American parents. Twenty-eight years old. Single. No people alive. Had no trade. Had travelled around the world and never worked when he could help it. Never worked in the country. Looked like a regular tramp and hard drinker.

No. 44.

Born in Newark, N. J. French parents. Twenty-four years old. Single. Had two sisters in Brooklyn. Had no regular trade but had been working for three weeks in a grocery store and thus had a room in the Army Hotel. Never worked in the country. Looked capable and intelligent.

No. 45.

Born in Brooklyn. American parents. Twenty-four years old. Single. Had people in Brooklyn who were helping him. Had no trade but had worked all his life at odd jobs. Could not work steadily because of bad habits. Never worked in the country. Looked like a hard drinker.

No. 46.

Born in Jersey City. Irish parents. Thirty-five years old. Single. Was a painter by trade but did not belong to the Union. Had been out of work three months. Some friends gave him clothes and a little money. Looked intelligent but dissipated.

No. 47.

Born in Brooklyn. Irish parents. Thirty years old. Single. Had no trade. Worked on a farm in Long Island and hoped to go to the country shortly. Had had no steady work the past Winter. Had been in the Army Industrial Home six times during the Winter. Looked shiftless and dissipated.

No. 48.

Born in Lowell, Mass. Italian parents. Twenty years old. Single. People lived in Lowell. Had no trade. Never worked in the country. Came to New York two weeks previously with a little money, but this was soon spent and he had walked the streets two nights. Entered the Army Hotel through charity. Had written home for money and expected to return there. His appearance was very good.

No. 49.

Born in New York. American parents. Forty years old. Married. Separated from his wife three months ago because of his drinking. Had no trade. Never worked in the country. Had been out of work three months. Picked up odd jobs now and then, and thus secured a bed. Looked like a hard drinker.

No. 50.

Born in Germany. Seventeen years old. Single. Had people in Germany who were unable to help him. Had been in this country nine months. Said he was on a farm in New York State but ran away. The Salvation Army was keeping him, and he worked a little around the Hotel. Looked like a promising boy but rather wild.

No. 51.

Born in Denver, Col. American parents. Twenty-three years old. Single. Had people at home who sent him money now and then. Was an iron-worker. Belonged to the Union, but said the Union had not helped him any. Had been out of work some time. Never worked in the country. Had travelled a good deal in the United States. Looked bright and promising.

No. 52.

Born in Davenport, Washington. Twenty-four years old. Single. Had people at home where he had sent for money. Had travelled widely. Came to New York five weeks ago from Panama where he had been working for eight months. Had to leave on account of sickness. Had $100.00 when he came to New York but spent nearly all on doctors bills. Still had a little left. Said he had worked a good deal on a farm. Looked capable and intelligent.

No. 53.

American, born in New York. Thirty years old. Single. People dead. Bartender. Did not belong to the Union. Was out of work for one month until two weeks previous to interview, when he got a job as bartender. Was still working and had a room at the Army Hotel. Said he would be all right it he could leave drink alone. He never worked in the country.

No. 54.

Born in New York. Irish parents. Twenty-eight years old. Single. Had quarrelled with his people who lived in New York. Painter by trade. Lost his membership in the Union because he did not pay his dues. Had had no steady work for a year, but had wandered all over the country doing very little work, but receiving aid from charitable societies. Said he liked the warm weather, so that he could sleep in the parks. Looked shiftless and a typical tramp.

No. 55.

Born in Norway. About thirty years old. Single. Had people in Norway who did not help him. Came to New York from his native land two months previously. A carpenter by trade. Was working in Jersey and lost position two weeks previously. Had money in his pocket and was evidently wise enough to keep it. Conversed in broken English. Said he worked in the country in Norway. Looked like a capable man.

No. 56.

Born in Scotland. Forty-five years old. Single. Came to this country with his people when he was nine years old. People had since died. Bookkeeper by trade. Had been out of work all Winter. The Scotch Aid Society was keeping him, giving him bed and meal tickets. Said he had received help from four different missions in New York. Looked incapable and shiftless. Never worked in the country.

No. 57.

Born in Jersey City. American parents. Twenty-eight years old. Single. Had no trade. Did not work if he could help it. Came here from the West by means of freight trains. Never worked in the country. Looked like a regular tramp.

No. 58.

Born in Chicago. Single. Thirty-years old. Had friends in Chicago who sent him a little money. Had no trade. Never did hard work. Got odd jobs and received aid from missions. Said he was a Christian and liked to attend meetings. Had a room in the Army Hotel. Said he had been staying there off and on for two years. Looked stupid and incapable.

No. 59.

Born in Denver, Col. Fifty years old. Single. Plumber by trade. Belonged to the Union but left eight months previously and had not paid his dues since. Was in business for himself at one time, but lost it through drink. Said he got help from the missions whenever he could. Never worked in the country. Hoped to go West again shortly. Looked feeble and dissipated.

No. 60.

American. Born in Springfield, Mass. Fifty-five years old. Single. Said his people in Springfield were wealthy but would have nothing to do with him. Had no trade. In New York all Winter. Had walked the streets a good many nights. Never worked in the country. Charity Organization Society had helped him, besides other organizations. Said he had consumption. Looked very weak and dissipated.

No. 61.

Born in America. Jewish parents. Twenty-six years old. Single. Stone-cutter by trade. Said he worked at the Insurance business at times. Had been out of work nearly two months. Never worked in the country. Looked bright and capable.

No. 62.

Born in Cleveland, Ohio. American parents. Twenty-six years old. Single. People lived in Cleveland, but did not help him. Had worked on a farm nearly all his life. Left the farm two years previously and had wandered most of the time since. He expected to be sent to the country by the Bowery Mission shortly. Looked shiftless but not dissipated.

No. 63.

Born in New York. American parents. About fifty years old. Married. Said his people were dead. Had no regular trade. Did office work, but was nearly always out of work. Said he was a Christian. He evidently followed the missions and "got saved" every time he needed help. Never worked in the country. Looked shiftless and inefficient.

No. 64.

Born in Brooklyn. English parents. Thirty years old. Married. Quarrelled with his wife five years previously and left her. Painter by trade. Did not belong to the Union. Had not worked all Winter. Said he had been all around the world and had beaten his way wherever he went. Had been in jail several times, for vagrancy and drunkness. Never worked in the country. Looked like a tramp.

No. 65.

Born in Maine. American parents. Twenty-four years old. Single. Had people in Maine from whom he expected help. Barber by trade. Came to New York three weeks previously. Met some friends on the Bowery and lost all his money. The Army was helping him. He had worked somewhat in the country. Looked very stupid.

No. 66.

Born in Scotland. About sixty years old. Single. Had no people. Had no trade. In this country for forty years. Out of work all Winter. The Scotch Aid Society had been keeping him now for three weeks. He never worked in the country. He looked like a regular vagrant.

No. 67.

Born in Boston. American parents. Twenty-four years old. Single. A waiter. Had wandered a good deal, and beaten his way by freight trains. Came to New York from the West one month previously. Had not worked since, but had been aided by the missions and the Army. Evidently did not like to work.

No. 68.

Born in Poughkeepsie, N. Y. Irish parents. About thirty-two years old. Single. Had no trade. Came to New York two weeks previously with some money which he got from his people. He had sent home for more. Worked somewhere in the country. Said he drank periodically and did not like to work steadily. Looked very shiftless.

No. 69.

Born in Ireland. Twenty-eight years old. Single. Had lost track of his people. Had been in this country eight years. Had no trade. Had had no steady work all Winter. Drank a good deal. Never worked in the country. Looked very wild.

No. 70.

Born in New Orleans. Spanish parents. About twenty years old. Single. Left home two years ago and took to life on the water. Left the boat in New York one month previously and had not worked since. Said he liked to sail and see the world. His people lived in New Orleans, and he expected help from them. Never worked in the country. Looked capable.

No. 71.

Born in New York. American parents. About thirty years old. Single. Had trade as a bartender. Belonged to the Union. Lost a steady job through drink three weeks ago. Was now working four hours a day. Had a room in the Army Hotel. Said he was going to change his line of business because he drank too much. His appearance was good. Never worked in the country.

No. 72.

Born in Germany. Looked like a Jew. About twenty-five years old. Single. Had no trade. Had been out of work three months. Was now selling old clothing and other things around the Army Hotel. Never worked in the country. Evidently lazy and incapable.

No. 73.

Born in Illinois. American parents. About twenty-eight years old. Single. Ran away from home and was ashamed to go back. Had no trade but had worked a good deal as cook on board ship. Had been out of work six weeks. Said he was sick and had about $200.00, but it did not last long. He was working round the Army Hotel a little every day, for which he got his bed and one meal ticket. Never worked in the country. Said he was going to join the navy. Looked bright and capable.

No. 74.

Born in Lithuania. Twenty-three years old. Single. People at home were poor. Had no trade. In New York three years. Out of work two months. Obtained clothes in various ways and sold them. Was not dissipated, but looked lazy. Never worked in the country.

No. 75.

Born in Yonkers, N. Y. American parents. About sixty-five years old. Single. Was an old sailor but had not been to sea for over a year. Was working two days a week as janitor. Said he had been a hard drinker in the past, but he did not drink much now. He looked aged, but still capable. Never worked in the country.

No. 76.

Born in Boston. Irish parents. About twenty-five years old. Single. Had no trade. People did not recognize him. Had travelled all over the country. Had been in jail twice. Never worked in the country. Looked like a tramp.

SOME FACTS BROUGHT OUT IN THE 76 HOTEL EXAMPLES.

Nationality. No. Percentage.

American parentage 35 .461

Irish parentage 20 .263

English and Scotch parentage 9 .119

German parentage 8 .105

Other countries 4 .052

Married men 7 .095

Single men 69 .905

Worked a little in country 13 .169

Worked considerably in country 5 .065

Men with regular trades 26 .342 [56]

Union men 4 .052

Men who looked efficient 15 .197

Men who looked semi-efficient 14 .184

Men who looked inefficient 47 .619

Ages.

15-20 4 .052

20-30 42 .553

30-40 16 .211

40-50 6 .079

50-60 7 .092

60-70 1 .013

Length of time out of work.

Less than 1 mo. 12 .157

More than 1 mo. 13 .171

More than 2 mos. 11 .145

More than 3 mos. 40 .527

FACTS BROUGHT OUT IN THE 109 INDUSTRIAL EXAMPLES

AND THE 76 HOTEL EXAMPLES COMBINED.

Nationality. No. Percentage.

American parentage 76 .411

Irish parentage 50 .270

German parentage 26 .141

English and Scotch parentage 18 .098

Italian parentage 4 .022

Swedish parentage 4 .038

Other countries, parentage 7 .20

Married men 24 .149

Single men 161 .851

Worked a little in country 29 .156

Worked considerably in country 12 .016

Men with regular trades 57 .309

Union men 10 .054

Men who looked efficient 53 .287

Men who looked semi-efficient 35 .189

Men who looked inefficient 97 .524

Ages.

15-20 6 .032

20-30 97 .525

30-40 39 .210

40-50 26 .140

50-60 50 .082

60-70 2 .011

Length of time out of work.

Less than 1 mo. 20 .108

More than 1 mo. 30 .163

More than 2 mos. 27 .145

More than 3 mos. 108 .584

FOOTNOTES:

[38] "How the Other Half Lives," p. 38.

[39] This differentiation is more pronounced in the United States, since the work has been extended here more than in other countries.

[40] For adverse criticism see "The Social Relief Work of the S. A.," p. 9.

[41] At the Burne St. Shelter, the largest in London, one large dormitory has 288 beds and another 265.

[42] For rooms, special rates are given by the week; from some of the examples given at the end of this chapter, it will be seen that these are occupied by men with partial or poorly paid employment.

[43] In London, the Army has a mattress factory which supplies its institutions.

[44] More headway is being made in this direction in the Industrial Homes where the population is more permanent. We found in one home in Chicago that the men were organized in the form of a club, and enjoyed social meetings together. Also, at the largest Industrial Home in London, called "The Spa Road Elevator," we found a regular cricket club organized which played cricket games with other clubs.

[45] Good examples of this are to be found in the Middlesex Street Hotel and the Burne Street Hotel, London. The former hotel is regularly provided, by a large

baker firm, with food, which is one day stale, for a very low figure.

[46] The higher class hotel for women is to be found in Los Angeles and Boston.

[47] From an interview with a leading officer.

[48] These exceptions are certain of the lower class hotels where attempts along this line seem to fail.

[49] See "How the Other Half Lives," Ch. VIII. See also "Social Relief Work of the S. A.," p. 10.

[50] See examples given at the end of this chapter, p. 77.

[51] See the tables, pp. 97 and 98, showing percentages of these men who had come from the country. For the work of Mr. Fox see p. 113.

[52] See examples of these men, p. 77 fl.

[53] See Giddings' "Principles of Sociology," p. 127.

[54] Some light may be thrown on this subject by a perusal of Mr. W. H. Dawson's book entitled "The German Workman," although conditions are evidently vastly different in this country and England from what they are in Germany.

[55] See examples numbered 4. 5. 9. 23 and others, on p. 78 and fl.

[56] While this percentage is larger than that in the Industrial Homes (see p. 62), 62 per cent. of the examples

in the Hotels having regular trades were dissipated, mostly victims of drink, as against 19 per cent. in the Industrial examples.

CHAPTER III.

The Farm Colonies of the Salvation Army.

So many times has the cry been raised "back to the land!", so optimistic have so many reformers become over the hope that the population could be diverted from the city to the country, and so loudly have certain enthusiasts prophesied a surely successful issue to colonizing enterprises, that the Salvation Army colonies form a very interesting and profitable field of investigation. What is needed is an experiment that will prove or disprove the prophesied success of taking the people back to the land. Once that is proved, with the great Northwest of America almost untouched, with immense tracts of good land in Africa and other continents, and with the United States about to open up millions of acres of land, made fertile by means of irrigation, we shall be ready to act and get rid of the surplus city population. But first we must have the proof, and the question before us is whether the Salvation Army has sufficiently proved the case.

The matter was agitated before the English Government to such an extent in 1905 that the Rhodes Trustees, contributing sufficient funds to cover the expense, the

Secretary of State for the Colonies nominated Mr. Rider Haggard, the novelist, to visit the United States and inspect the three Salvation Army colonies there, to make a report on the same, and to include in this report any practical suggestions which might occur to him. The following words were used in the letter of commission: "It appears to the Secretary of State that if these experiments are found to be successful, some analogous system might to great advantage be applied in transferring the urban population of the United Kingdom to different parts of the United Kingdom." [57]

Mr. Haggard visited the three colonies in the United States, and made a report to the English Government, favoring strongly the movement, and recommending that the Government take it up, provide the capital and utilize all ready existing organizations, such as the Salvation Army, in carrying out its scheme. The matter was referred by the Government to the Departmental Committee, who, after reviewing it and looking into the question in 1906, issued a long report in which they discountenanced Mr. Haggard's scheme on the ground that:

1. It was better for settlers from England to be scattered about with experienced farmers as neighbors than to be placed in a number together.

2. The Salvation Army or any similar organization was not a desirable management for a colony dependent on money advanced by the Imperial Government.

3. That Ft. Romie and Ft. Amity, the American farm colonies of the Salvation Army, were not precedents upon which a large scheme of colonization could be based. [58]

The Committee gave reasons for arriving at the above conclusions, into which, for the present, we need not enter, but their conclusions are suggestive, and may be borne in mind while we make our study of the subject.

Gen. Booth, in his plans as outlined in "Darkest England," provided for three main divisions of the work for the unemployed poor, viz., the City Colony, the Country Colony and the Over-sea Colony, signifying by these terms the City Industrial Work, the Country Industrial Colony, and the Farm Colony. [59] The last named was to be on a larger scale on some Colonial territory of England. This division has tended to persist in the United States, and this country has been the field for special experiments along this line. There are three Colonies in the United States: Fort Herrick, situated near Cleveland, Ohio; Fort Amity, situated in Southeast Colorado, and Ft. Romie, which is located at Soledad in the Salinas Valley, California. At first there was no differentiation between these Colonies, but latterly, the Colony at Ft. Herrick, the smallest of the three, has been managed as an Industrial Colony, and the other two have continued as regular Farm Colonies. The plan of "Commander" Booth-Tucker, in charge of the Salvation Army in the United States from 1896 until 1904, and the originator of these Colonies, was, in brief, as he states it, to take the waste labor in families, and place it upon the waste land by means of waste capital, and thereby to convert this trinity of waste into a unity of production. [60] His waste labor was the family struggling in the crowded city; his waste land, the large tracts of public land about to be opened up by irrigation; and his waste capital, if such a term can be used, was the capital lying idle, or at least, making 2½ or 3 per cent., when according to his estimate, it could yield 5 per cent. The principles which he laid down were as follows:

1. There must be sufficiency of capital.

2. The land must be carefully selected and laid out.

3. The colonists must be well selected.

4. There must be able supervision.

5. The principle of home ownership must be followed.

6. God must be recognized.

From our investigations at Ft. Romie and Ft. Amity, we arrived at the conclusion that No. 4 and No. 6 were the only ones thoroughly carried out; that there was a weakness in the amount of capital (Prin. No. 1); that an unfortunate selection of land was made (Prin. No. 2); that the successful colonists did not entirely represent the class from which we should wish them to be taken (Prin. No. 3); and that ownership gave way largely to a system of renting-out by the Army (Prin. No. 5). For verification of this, see the typical cases at the end of the chapter.

Commander Booth-Tucker advanced the argument, which is sound, to the effect that, when entire families were taken from the city and placed on the land, the tendency to return to the city would be overcome. It has been the experience of philanthropists, that when single men and women were transferred from the city to the country, they always tended to return, the reason being due to an acquired fondness of the individual for intimate association with his fellows, [61] but when a man has his wife and children, together with a plot of land and a home which he may call his own, the attraction toward the city is overcome, by a stronger one which keeps him where he is. Of course, this would answer for the one generation only.

Leaving out the small colony at Ft. Herrick, Ohio, which was changed to an Industrial Colony, and which is considered in the chapter on the Industrial Work, let us examine more closely the Farm Colonies at Ft. Amity, Col., and Ft. Romie, Cal. The larger enterprise was set on foot in Colorado, in 1898, where a tract of 2,000 acres was secured at a cost of $46,000.00. In this year, fourteen families were brought from Chicago and placed on the bare, unimproved prairie, where, however, there was abundant water supply carried by a large irrigation company. These colonists were all family men with two exceptions, and nine of the heads of families had either been on farms or had worked on farms in the past. [62] They were in narrow circumstances financially, and the transportation expenses of all except one of these families were paid by the Army. With this migration as a basis, the number of colonists was greatly increased by families from different cities and also from the surrounding country, until in 1905, there were thirty-eight families. Several were brought to the Colony as experienced men to act as pace-setters for the others. [63] Some came with a small amount of capital.

Owing to the fact that the land was covered by a heavy sod which needed considerable working, no crops were raised the first year, and only fair crops the second. During the first year, the colonists were supported by cash loans which were charged against them. After the first two years, crops were good [64], and the outlook was promising, in spite of certain insect pests, but after about seven years a great difficulty showed itself. The land on which the Colony was located was alkali land, and bottom land, without any drainage. The result of constant irrigation was that the alkali rose to the surface in larger and larger quantities, until no good crop could be raised. The only salvation was to drain the land and thus rid it of the blighting alkali. This meant an expense of from $30.00 to $40.00 an acre. At the present time draining is being rapidly pushed forward and is proving very beneficial, but it can be easily seen what a discouragement the alkali has proved to the colonists, and what an additional expense is laid upon them and the Colony; an expense which it will take years of good crops to overcome. [65]

Up to 1905, about eighteen families, not satisfied with the results obtained, had moved away, and their places had been filled by others. A very few of the departing families moved because of ill-health; some thought that they could do better elsewhere as farmers; some even had considerable money as a result of their holdings in the Colony [66]. Since 1905, there has been a good deal of changing, and at present a large part of the Colony land is rented out by the Army to settlers; some being from the country, and some from the city [67]. A small number of the old pioneer colonists still remain and have done well with their holdings in spite of all difficulties. [68]

The Army stated in 1905, that the financial standing of this Colony showed a net loss to the Army of $23,111.50, and a gain to the colonists of $37,943.77. It considered its loss a cheap price for the experience gained, but thought that it had erred in giving the colonists too liberal terms. [69] By this time the loss to the Army is considerably greater, owing to the increased expense of drainage. [70]

At the present time (January, 1908), the population of this Colony is about 200. Nearly all the land is occupied in one way or another, either by colonists who own, or partially own, their land, or by renters, who are also called colonists. Several homes are vacant, but it is expected that they will be filled by renters before the Spring season opens. The little village consists of several stores, a blacksmith shop, a substantial railroad depot, a post office, a small hotel and a school house. A good many of the homes are built of stone, quarried on the Colony, and present a good appearance. Up on the higher land is situated a large stone structure, built by the colonists at an expense to the Army of $18,000.00, and first used as an orphanage, then as a sanitorium, and now abandoned. Irrigation ditches with a good flow of water are in evidence, and preparations for draining the land are under way. That this is necessary is forced upon us by the many white patches scattered here and there where the water, having evaporated, has left the destructive alkali salt on the surface of the ground.

When we come to consider the other Farm Colony, Ft. Romie, situated at Soledad, Cal., in the beautiful Salinas Valley, we receive a more favorable impression, although we find that the Colony here has had many difficulties with which to contend. The Colony is smaller than that at Ft. Amity, but the land is better. The original 500 acres has been increased by the addition of a lease of 150 acres with the option of buying. In the year 1898, eighteen families were taken from the poor of San Francisco and placed upon the Colony, but unforeseen conditions prevailed, and, as a result, but one of these families remains to-day. [71] The great mistake was made of settling colonists upon land which needed irrigation, before that irrigation was provided. This mistake was brought out the more vividly, in that the three first years of the Colony's existence were years of drought, bringing evil to most parts of the State, and especially to that land which, like the Colony land, only received a slight rain-fall at best. The result of the first years of this experiment, then, was an abandoning of the land by the colonists, and a loss to the Army of $27,000.00.

The experiment was continued, however, but with very different conditions. An excellent irrigation system was established, and a new lot of settlers brought to the Colony; not, this time, from the city, but from the surrounding country. These people were poor, but accustomed to the land. The result, as might be expected this time, was more favorable. It was stated in 1905 that no colonists had left since 1901. [72] In May, 1903, there were nineteen families ranged according to nationality as follows:—Thirteen American; Two Scandinavian; One Finn; One German-Swiss; One Dutch and one Italian. There are now twenty-five families, and about one hundred and forty-five persons on the Colony. The nucleus of a town is to be seen with two or three stores, a blacksmith shop, and a good sized Town Hall. Near the Colony is a school house with an attendance of about fifty children, most of them being colonists' children.

An irrigation plant has been established and is now owned and worked by the colonists, formed in a joint-stock company. The colonists raise beets, potatoes, alfalfa, fruits of different kinds, and stock. A large part of their income is derived from the dairying industry. They ship their cream to a creamery at Salinas, about twenty-five miles distant.

Much could be said about the healthy appearance and happy life of the members of this Colony, but as they have not been brought from the unhealthy, squalid misery of the city, this is not of so much interest. The women work in the vegetable gardens and with the stock, as well as in the home; and the older children help their parents.

Along the lines of co-operation, in both colonies there are interesting features. At stated intervals, the colonists meet in the form of a Farmers' Club, and discuss questions relative to the success of their individual farms and to the Colony as a whole. They also have lecturers come from a distance to address them on the latest phases of horticulture, agriculture, fertilization and irrigation. The colonists also embark in business enterprises like the stock company formed in the California Colony for the control and management of the irrigation plant. In this plant, one of the colonists is engineer, and another the superintendent of water supply. Another important institution of this same Colony is the Rochdale store, which does most of the retail business in the Colony. This store, in its management and organization, follows the co-operative Rochdale system, which has attained strength in England and is growing in the United States. The store is incorporated in the State of California as a co-operative corporation, and holds a membership in the State Rochdale Wholesale Co. It has already extended beyond the limits of the Colony and counts among its members others than colonists. The colonists also take active interest in local affairs of all kinds. In one colony, the rural mail carrier is a colonist, and the school teacher the wife of a colonist. At Ft. Amity, a colonist is now sheriff of the County for the second time.

Social and religious life is also fostered in the Colonies. A variety of religious sects is represented, and no compulsion is exercised towards any one of them. At Ft. Romie the Army has an organized corps, which holds meetings once in the week and once on Sunday, also having a Sunday school for the children. At Ft. Amity similar conditions prevail. On both colonies a good moral influence is found and there are no evil surroundings; hence in neither colony is there a local officer of the law. In the contract which every colonist signs on taking his land there is a temperance clause to this effect:

"And party of the second part hereby agrees to and with party of the first part that, in consideration of the benefits derived from this contract, he will not bargain, sell, barter or trade upon said land any intoxicating liquors, or otherwise dispose of as beverages any intoxicants, at any place upon said premises or any part thereof, or permit the selling of the same, or any illegal traffic or any act or acts prohibited by law."

The same clause goes on to provide for the return of the land to the Army in case of its being violated.

From this brief description it is seen that much of the success of these colonies must rest on the management. The manager must be large-hearted and broad-minded. He must be supervisor, instructor, moderator, counsellor and friend. The Army has been very fortunate in placing fit men in these positions, and if in other things it had been equally fortunate, its colonies would have made a better showing.

As regards the financial methods of the Army in dealing with the colonists, the following extract from a memorandum of information issued by the Ft. Romie Colony, California, gives typical information.

1. Land: Twenty acres of land are sold to each colonist. The price of unimproved land at this date, 1904, is $100.00 per acre. This price, however, is liable to be increased at any time. [73]

2. Buildings: Houses, barns and other buildings are constructed by the colonists. Materials are furnished in

quantities by the Army according to the size of the colonist's family, somewhat after the following schedule. For a family with one or two small children, a two-room house, about 14×24 outside measurement, for which we appropriate not over $125.00. This is to include a small barn or shed for horses, cows, etc. For a family with three or four small children, a three-room house about 18×24, costing with barn, etc., not over $175.00. For a larger family, perhaps a four or five-room house, limiting the appropriation for the same to $225.00. Colonists can suit themselves as to the style of the house, but must satisfy the manager that it can be erected within the limits of the appropriation named. The colonist can add to the size of the house as he gets on his financial feet.

3. Terms: On land breaking and other permanent land improvements, the colonists are given 20 years' time. The principal and interest are payable in installments each year.

4. Outfit: To colonists unable to purchase them, the Army furnishes the necessary implements and stock, consisting of the following: Team of horses, cow, hogs, chicken, seed, etc., secured by chattel mortgage. The interest on outfit and loans is fixed at 6 per cent. It is expected that the principal and interest will be repaid in installments each year. All outfits and loans are to be repaid within five years. [74]

We have briefly outlined the most prominent features of the Farm Colonies, but the final questions now arise, is the movement sound; what does it signify, and what development does the future hold for it? For one thing we must not be led astray by the statements of the Army. The continued existence of the colonies, in the face of great difficulties, through the term of eight or nine years they have been carried on, is not in itself an argument for the soundness of the movement. From ocean to ocean and throughout the world, the Army has advertised its success in colonizing enterprises, and hence it had a set purpose in maintaining and continuing its colonies, even though they should be failures from our point of view, and even though they should not fulfil the purpose originally intended by the Army itself. As has been remarked with regard to the industrial colonies, so here, we would emphasize the fact that the Army has no need to fear acknowledgement that the colonies have not been successful, because it has other credit upon which to depend for its reputation for usefulness. After looking at it from all sides, we come to the conclusion that the two experiments considered in these pages do not justify an extension of this work. This conclusion is based on several reasons:

1. Many of the successful colonists are not men who needed help the most, and many are not from the City at all.

2. The colonies have been, and are, an undue expense to the organization.

3. The same amount of energy and money would be more beneficial to the unemployed if used along other lines.

4. The principles advanced as essential by the originators of the movement were only partially carried out. [75]

Our first reason is based partly on personal investigation, and partly on the statements of the Army itself. [76] There are, as will be seen from examples given, certain places where families from the city without previous experience have made a success of the colonies, but these are greatly in the minority [77]. If, in the case of the California Colony at Fort Romie, when seventeen out of the original number of families taken from the city, left on account of the lack of water, the next group of settlers had again been chosen from the city, after water had been secured, a more conclusive experiment would have resulted, but instead, the second group were, "farmers by profession." [78] This looks as though the Army itself at that time doubted the ability of the city families to succeed on the land. At any rate, the fact that the majority of the families at the present time on the colonies are not from the city at all, shows that, as an experiment of removing the surplus population of the city to the country, the colonies are a failure. But further, when we take the minority, the families now in the colonies who came from the city, we find that, in most cases, they are not people who needed help the most, and those who have succeeded on the colonies, have succeeded because of elements in their character which would have led them to succeed in the long run anywhere, with favorable environment. In this case then, the only advantage in taking these people from the city was to leave more room there for somebody else, and this is not much of an advantage, since that "somebody else" is quite likely to come from the country to the city, and thus not be one of the city's submerged ones at all. Again, if, as we have just stated, men succeed in the country because of the same elements of character which would lead them to succeed anywhere, then the reason for their failing to succeed in the city would lie in an unfavorable environment, and to change their environment, it is not necessary to carry on a system of paternalistic colonies. This leads us to the question of assisted emigration, which we will discuss in connection with our third objection to the colonies.

As regards the second reason, that of undue expense, Mr. Haggard in 1905, found a loss to the Army of $50,000. While, since that time, in the case of the California Colony, there has been no further loss, yet in the case of the colony in Colorado, there has been much expenditure which should be added to the original loss. The Army states that it has been too liberal in its dealings with its colonists, but we note that, in spite of its liberality, there has been a constant tendency for the colonists to leave, hoping to do better elsewhere. [79] The Army might reply that this is no argument, and that the fact that they were able to leave with funds on hand was in itself a proof of liberality on the Army's part, but to prove the success of its experiment, it must show that those who have left have done better elsewhere, and not drifted back once more to the city. The Army might further state that in future a better selection of land might be made, and that other unfavorable things might be avoided, but we are dealing here with these two colonies and not future experiments. As regards such, there would always be unforeseen difficulties of every kind. [80]

Coming to the third reason for our conclusion, the reason that money might be expended in other ways with greater advantage to the unemployed, and with greater relief to the congestion of cities, we refer again to the recommendations of the Departmental Committee appointed by the English government to consider Commissioner Haggard's report. [81] In their report they recommend a system of emigration from the city to the English possessions, such as Canada, aided by the government, in preference to the system of colonization. With this we agree. A man once transported from the city and then thrown on his own resources in a favorable rural environment, will be more likely to succeed than a man who is taken out with a number of others to form a colony. The man left to his own resources will rise to the occasion, as so many have done in both Canada and the United States, who have migrated from city to country and made successful farmers and citizens, while, on the other hand, the man who feels dependent on an organization, which is responsible to the public for his success, and its own, will blame it for his own lack of efficiency. The Army itself claims a successful work done along the lines of emigration. In 1905, through the agency of the Army, 2,500 men were sent out from London to Canada. This number has since increased every year until in 1907 over 15,000 men were sent out. Many other emigration societies have been very successful in this work. [82] The emigrants sent out with some assistance, in many cases, gain new ambitions in life and make pronounced successes on the new soil. As regards the cost, the following quotation may be submitted. "The cost of emigration to Canada from England does not amount to more than £10 a head, and some of the societies, especially those maintained by women, seem to be successful in securing repayment of at least a part of the money advanced. In other words, $300,000.00, which Mr. Rider Haggard assumes as a necessary sum for forming a colony of 1,500 families, would enable at least 6,000 families to go out as emigrants." [83] With regard to conditions in the large cities of the United States and other countries, we believe that the same arguments would apply, and that, in every case, assisted emigration will be found far more feasible and beneficial than any system of colonization. Again, for reasons already given, in addition to there being six thousand families aided by emigration, for the same sum as fifteen hundred families could be by colonization, the relief given would be far preferable. In other words, emigration has been proved successful, while colonization has not.

Coming back to the conclusions reached by Mr. Haggard on his recommendations to the English government: Mr. Haggard, after stating that the two experiments, outside of a slight failure of finance, seemed to him to be eminently successful, says that, given certain requisites,

"It will, I consider, be strange if success is not attained even in the case of poor persons taken from the cities, provided that they are suited in character, the victims of misfortune and circumstances rather than of vice, having had some acquaintance or connection with the land in their past life, and having also an earnest desire to raise themselves and their children in the world."

Now two of the "requisites" he mentions are, "that the land should be cheap as well as suitable" and "that markets also with accessibility and convenience of location should be borne in mind," two rather difficult requisites to be found together. Again, in the above quotation he lays down other provisos; among these being one that the people selected should have had some acquaintance or connection with the land in their past lives, a rather indefinite proviso in itself, but, from a list of poor men out of work or in irregular or casual employment in London and the other large cities in England in 1901 and 1906, compiled by Mr. Wilson Fox, we find that out of a total of 8,793 such men, ninety per cent were town born. [84] We also find in New York City in the spring of 1908, that out of a total of 185 destitute men, about eighty per cent were town born. [85] That then leaves ten per cent in the case of England and twenty per cent in the case of New York City from which to select or choose the ones needed for a colonizing enterprise.

Mr. Fox has also shown in his investigations:

1. That the countrymen who migrate to London are mainly the best youth of the villages.

2. That the incomers usually get the pick of the posts, especially outdoor trades.

3. Country immigrants do not to any considerable extent directly recruit the town unemployed who are, in the main, the sediment deposited at the bottom of the scale, as the physique and power of application of the town population tends to deteriorate. [86]

The conclusion is then, that it would be difficult to get the men according to Mr. Haggard's requirements, and difficult to get the land according to his requirements, and even if such were obtained, for reasons already stated there is no justification for a large colonizing enterprise in the two experiments described in this chapter.

Examples of Colonists taken from Ft. Amity by the author in January, 1908.

No. 1.

Elderly man. Widower. Had three grown-up children in the Colony at various times. Had one son a colonist with farm of his own. Was not a Salvationist. Came from Chicago where he was a tailor. Had a farm near the railroad depot which he considered valuable. Had two small houses. Rented one. Raised alfalfa. Was sole agent for a coal company. Claimed he made $1,500.00 last year, mostly in the coal business. Said draining now being done on the Colony was very expensive. Considered the Colony a good thing.

No. 2.

Middle aged man. Married. One child. Had experience in the country before coming to the Colony. Had forty acres of Colony land which he had rented, and which he wished to sell at $106.00 per acre. Had mostly worked for the railroad in the station office. Wished to leave the Colony. Said he could not raise a vegetable garden owing to alkali and insect pests.

No. 3.

A new man. About thirty years old. One year out from Chicago, where he worked at different trades. Had wife and one child. Rented a house on the Colony and worked in one of the Colony stores. Had no money saved and saw no immediate chance of betterment. Liked the country better than the city, because his wife had better health.

No. 4.

Young married man. No children. Son of a Colonist and married to a daughter of a Colonist, whose father was sheriff of the County. Had good looking cottage and barns. Was doing well.

No. 5.

About fifty years old. Salvation Army officer. In the Colony six years. Had son twenty-one, and together they worked a farm of sixty acres. He owned twenty and rented forty. His life was despaired of by the doctors, but he was enjoying good health at time of interview. Doing well financially.

No. 6.

About forty-five. Original Colonist. Married. Had four children. Came from Chicago, where he was a carpenter. Owned land in the Colony which he rented out. Ran a hardware store in the Colony and was partner in the Colony bank. Had property valued at $5,000.00. Had no capital when he came to the Colony.

No. 7.

About forty-eight years old. Original Colonist. Married and had nine children. Was railroad clerk in Chicago at $12.00 per week. Owned a corner lot on the town site where he ran a grocery store. Had property in Chicago worth $1,000.00 when he came to the Colony. Was worth $8,000.00 at time of interview.

No. 8.

A farmer, from surrounding country, induced by Colony management to invest in Colony land and tract as a "pace-setter" to the other colonists. Thus secured forty acres at $70.00 per acre. Had introduced the sheep industry. Bought up young lambs in Mexico, fattened them, and sold at a profit. Had been two years on the Colony. Made $5,000.00 net, per year. Had four thousand sheep.

No. 9.

Middle aged man. Married. Original colonist. Was expressman in Chicago, but previous to coming to the Colony had to leave family and go to work in the woods while the wife worked. Had taken out a government homestead outside of the Colony. Gave up his holdings on the Colony and was working as farm boss for a neighboring farmer while his wife ran a boarding house.

No. 10.

Scotchman. About fifty years old. Married. Had five children. In the Colony for six years. Arrived there with $25.00. Was carpenter in Chicago. Was worth $1,000.00 when interviewed. Was arranging to sell his holdings and go away, as he thought he could do better elsewhere.

No. 11.

About forty-five years old. Belonged to the Army. Married. One child. Came from Baltimore, Md., where he worked as a teamster. The Army paid family's fare to the Colony. Made a failure of his holding on the Colony and was making a bare living by running the Colony hotel and doing teaming. His failure was due to alkali and insect pests. His wife was sick before coming, but became better and was evidently the more efficient member of the partnership.

No. 12.

Thirty-five years old. Married. Two children. Brother of Army officer and son of example No. 1. In the Colony eight years. Used to be street-car conductor in Chicago. Gave up one holding in the Colony on account of alkali and took another, where he was doing well at time of interview.

No. 13.

About forty years old. Married. Came from the country. Rented a house on the Colony and worked as a section-hand on the railroad.

FOOTNOTES:

[57] "The Poor and the Land." Introduction, p. VI.

[58] "Report of Departmental Committee," pp. 8, 9, 10.

[59] "William Booth," p. 83.

[60] "The S. A. in the U. S.," p. 15.

[61] See Giddings' "Principles of Sociology," p. 291.

[62] "The Poor and the Land," p. 75.

[63] See example No. 8 at the end of the chapter, p. 115.

[64] About this time, Mr. Curtis, describing the colony in the Chicago Record, said "There is no neater group of houses in Colorado, and no more contented community in the world. Nearly every one has written to friends urging them to join the next colony that comes out, and thus I judge they are enthusiastic over their success and the pleasures they enjoy."

[65] See principle No. 2, p. 101.

[66] "The Poor and the Land," p. 78.

[67] See principle No. 5, p. 101.

[68] See several examples at the end of this chapter, p. 137.

[69] "The Poor and the Land," p. 82.

[70] See principle No. 1, p. 101.

[71] "The Poor and the Land," p. 39.

[72] See Pamphlet, "Review of Salvation Army Land Colony in California."

[73] The price of land at Ft. Amity would be different, and there, too, the Army sometimes rents to the colonists an additional acreage.

[74] "Memorandum of Information Respecting the Salvation Army Colony at Ft. Romie, California."

[75] For these principles see p. 101 of this chapter.

[76] See "The Poor and the Land," p. 40 and fl.

[77] See examples at end of chapter.

[78] See "The Poor and the Land," p. 47.

[79] See the "Poor and the Land," p. 82.

[80] See "Report of Departmental Committee," p. 14 and fl.

[81] Ibid.

[82] Mr. John Manson in his book "The Salvation Army and the Public," p. 133 and following, states that in this work the Army has merely acted the part of a business agency. We think that he has ground for this statement, but we also think that the Army would be far more useful along these lines than an ordinary business agency.

[83] See Report of Departmental Committee, p. 6.

[84] See Report of Departmental Committee, p. 3.

[85] See tables p. 98 of this book.

[86] See Report of Departmental Committee, p. 30.

CHAPTER IV.

The Salvation Army Slum Department.

So much has been written on the question of the slums in the past few years; so many settlements, evening recreation centers, summer playgrounds, clubs, visiting nurses' associations, and kindergarten associations have been organized; so much has been done by tenement house commissions and tenement laws; so many churches have turned from their original efforts to the slums; that we wonder why so little is heard of what the Army, the organization supposed especially to represent the poor, is doing in this direction. To tell the truth, if we go down into the slums, either those of Deptford, Whitechapel, or of Westminster, in London; or those of the Jewish, the Italian, the Negro, or the Irish quarters in New York, or those of the Slav or Jewish quarters in Chicago, expecting to find there the work of the Army much in evidence, we shall be disappointed. What slum work is done by the Army in these densely populated corners is done with love and earnest hearts, with sacrifice and the best of intentions; but apparently it does not bear fruit in the same proportion as does the work of the settlement, whether church settlement or secular, or in the same proportion as many of the kindergartens, summer playgrounds and evening recreation centers. Nevertheless, the slum post of the Army is doing valuable work and should be supported.

A sweeping tenement house reform can do more than any number of settlements; a settlement can do more than the Army slum post; but neither the tenement reform nor the settlement does the work that a slum post does. Probably the work done by other organizations most nearly allied to that of the Army slum post is that done by the various organizations of church deaconesses, which have been growing rapidly in late years, in which women are employed by the churches to visit the poor in their homes, and nurse the sick, besides other duties. If we depend or count largely on the Army slum work to reform the slums, we shall be disappointed in learning that, after years of successful growth in the Industrial and Social Departments, the Army has but twenty slum posts in the United States [87], some of these being very small, and that it has no large number in other countries. Such as it is, the work is well worth while. But let us examine its origin, present status and the reason for its relatively small growth.

In the beginning of the Army movement, Mrs. Booth, the late wife of General Booth, supplemented her husband's work by a personal visitation of the people in their homes. She proved the utility of this work and also its place among the works of women. From her early efforts has sprung the more widely organized department of slum work.

The slum work may be divided into three divisions: visitation work, the slum nursery, and the maintenance of the slum post. Wearing a humbler garb, even, than the regular Army uniform, the lassies start out on their daily tours of visitation. They take care of the sick, and at the same time, they clean the home and put everything in order. Often they come upon cases of need and of want, and then they provide the little necessaries: a sack of coal, a supply of food, or some needed clothing. They take the children from the worn-out woman and amuse and instruct them, while the mother does her work; and, wherever they go, although most plainly dressed, they are clean and neat, and they strive to make everything else clean and neat.

While this visitation work is going on, another most urgent need is being supplied by the slum nursery. Here the mother can leave her children in the morning, when she goes to her work, and find them safely waiting for her in the evening, clean and happy. A charge of five cents per day is made to cover the expense of feeding the children. During the day they are well cared for, the younger ones properly nursed, and the older ones taught simple little kindergarten games and songs. Sometimes children are brought here and never called for again, in which case the Army lassies in charge must find some permanent home for them, but this does not often happen, as the mothers of the children are usually known by the Army workers. At the slum nursery in Cincinnati there is also a free clinic, where sick women and children go for treatment. Two of the most efficient physicians of the city furnish free aid, and the medicines necessary are provided.

In addition to the visitation work and the nursery, the maintenance of the slum post means the keeping of slum quarters and a slum hall. The "quarters" are the two or more rooms where the lassies live, and they are located where most can be accomplished in the way of example and influence. The hall is for the carrying on of slum meetings, for these are regularly held. In these meetings the roughest crowd of men, women and children is awed into respect and reverence by the simple slum lassies with their songs and music. Again, in this little hall, the children of the neighborhood are gathered in a Sunday School and taught by the slum officers. It is a most interesting spectacle to watch these children. Many different nationalities are represented, the dark races and the light. As children, these nationalities mingle together more freely than in adult life.

A special aspect of the slum post is the distribution of charitable relief to the needy. It is specially situated, and has advantages for this purpose; hence it becomes the distributing depot for bread, soup and coal in winter, and ice in summer. For instance, from one slum post in New York during the winter of 1907-8, 2,800 loaves of bread were given out in one week, and for some months, an average of from 300 to 1,000 loaves, besides an average of two tons of coal per week. Some of this, naturally, would go to the undeserving, but the slum officers, as a rule, know the people of their immediate neighborhood, and can exercise due discretion.

The failure of the Army slum work to increase in the same proportion as its other branches of the social work, and its non-existence in many quarters of our cities where it is most needed, is due to two causes. One is the fact that the Army slum post, more than the Army industrial home or the Army hotel, is a religious institution, and is continually advertising and pressing on the public its peculiar doctrines. The slum officers are imbued with the idea that personal salvation according to the doctrines of the Army is the all-essential need. They would not be engaged in this work themselves were it not for the hold these doctrines have upon them. The slum post holds its regular meetings, exhorting its hearers to get "saved," in its own original way. At Sunday School, the children are taught that certain things are wrong and sinful, and these very things are common-place in their own homes though, possibly some of them of not much detriment. But, in a community almost entirely Catholic or Jewish, such aggressive evangelism is not likely to increase the influence of its advocates. Many settlements have learned with grief, this very same lesson. Another reason for the lack of success is the mental calibre of those engaged in the work. However, the devotion and self-sacrifice of the Army slum sisters is one of the most touching and sublime elements of the slums, and it is all the more touching when it is to some extent misdirected and misplaced. To see the tact, patience and perseverance of these "Slum Angels" as they are often called, is a divine object lesson in itself, and much of their work is not done in vain, as many would testify.

A useful experiment is under way at one former slum post, 94 Cherry Street, New York City. In place of the old building formerly rented by the Army here and used as a slum post, the Army has built a commodious six-story building, which it calls a settlement. One floor is given to a hall and parlor. Two floors are given over to rooms to be used as class, club and kindergarten rooms. One floor is fitted up with a dining room and kitchen, and another with a large dormitory and living room, to be used as a Girls' Home. On the roof, preparations are under way for a roof garden and play-ground, while washing facilities are provided in the basement, where poor mothers can bring their clothes and wash them. Already the New York

Kindergarten Association has two kindergartners busy here. Two sewing classes, averaging thirty-five members, are organized. Mother's meetings are held, and a regular Army Corps is organized, consisting of sixty members. This settlement may prove an auspicious advance of the Army along these lines.

To sum up, the Army Slum Department is doing valuable work in the slums, tending the sick, exercising and bringing out some of the better traits of humanity, and offering relief in times of need; but it suffers from an over-desire to spread its own peculiar doctrines of salvation, and from the lack of grasping the whole situation which is characteristic of its workers.

FOOTNOTES:

[87] This number has continued the same for five years.

CHAPTER V.

The Salvation Army Rescue Department.

In the United States and Great Britain, the question of the social evil has never been thoroughly investigated and faced systematically as a whole. In some of the large cities in the United States, notably in Chicago and New York, the question has been taken up in various ways by different reform societies. Probably the best investigation made thus far has been the work of the Committee of Fifteen, in New York City, which issued its report in the year 1902, but the problem does not appear to have been faced by us as a nation as it might have been. Other countries, especially France, have paid a great deal of attention to this form of vice. Nearly every phase of the question has been examined by some French investigator and reported on, but when we look for reports or investigations on the part of American or English students, we find very little of value.

As regards the United States, all attempts at reaching a true estimate of the extent of this evil have failed. Apparently, there is no way of obtaining such information. We have seen estimates regarding some of the cities in past years, and such estimates are given as 40,000 prostitutes for New York City, [88] 30,000 for Chicago and 35,000 for San Francisco. But these figures have evidently been derived in a very unscientific way. The evil is probably worse in the Western states than in the Eastern, but we are not satisfied of the accuracy of such estimates as 35,000 for San Francisco and only 30,000 for Chicago.

The work known as the Rescue Work of the Salvation Army is, to a certain extent, related to the Slum Work. The slum officers can often work hand-in-hand with the Rescue officers, inasmuch as their field is often on the same or adjoining territory. At the same time, it is essential that the Rescue officer be more highly specialized than the slum worker. During the past few years the percentage of successful cases of reform brought about by the Army Rescue Homes has reached as high as 80 or 85%, according to the Army's statistics. They, however, are unable to keep in touch with all the girls sent out, and hence this percentage would not be final, but even allowing 25% off for failures not known to the Army, it is doubtful if there is any other reform agency along this line which is as successful as is this force of trained rescue workers. [89] In the United States this force works in conjunction with twenty-two Rescue Homes scattered throughout the States. These homes are especially fitted for the work, some having been built for the purpose. There are work rooms for the girls, where they can do sewing and laundry work. There is a reading room and sitting room, dining room, and different dormitories and sleeping apartments. Then special facilities are provided for the care of babies in the way of proper nurseries.

There are two ways in which these girls come under the influence of the Homes and Rescue workers: either the girls come voluntarily to the Homes, expressing their desire to leave this form of life for a better one, or they are brought to the Home by the direct influence and touch of the Rescue officer. These Rescue officers make regular tours through the districts where the girls are to be found. They watch their opportunities, and whenever they think it wise, they speak to the girls personally. When this is not possible, they make an advance by way of literature. One method is to open up a conversation by means of a little card, upon which is printed the address of the Rescue Home, and the offer of help to any girl who is in trouble of any sort. Some of the officers tell us that they get to know the faces of the girls through their regular tours, and whenever a new girl comes they are able to recognize her at once, both by her features and her actions. In this way there have been some instances of real prevention without the need of any curative means whatever; instances where young girls have been rescued from the very brink of their evil fate. One way of reaching the girls is visitation and nursing when they are sick. Another way is through the police courts. In some of the latter a woman Army officer is in regular attendance, and the judge frequently hands certain cases over to her charge.

Many of the girls received into the Home have had no practical training in life; many, very little moral training, and in the case of those who have had good training in earlier years, the life they have been leading has so undermined their old ideals, that the training must be repeated. Hence, the aim of the Home is two-fold. First, the aim is to lay a strong foundation morally. When the girls reach the Home, in most cases they are already penitent, and ready for a change, but to make such a complete change as is necessary to lead them back to a normal life means the individual revolution of desire and interest. Here is where the importance of the moral influence of the Home is realized. Step by step the girl is led on by the simple teaching of Christian and social ideals, until in reality she is a changed individual. Often she looks back on her past life with such repugnance and shrinking, that her only desire becomes that of doing something to retrieve her past, and she becomes an active agent in the betterment of the conditions of other girls around her.

Meanwhile, the second aim of the Rescue Home is being realized. The girls are taught the means of practical livelihood. They are instructed in cooking, the care of the kitchen and nursery, and general housekeeping. Sewing is made a prominent feature, and in every Home a laundry is maintained, where the girls do their own washing and sometimes outside washing. In some Homes the fund realized from the laundry and from the sale of clothing made by the girls is quite a help toward defraying the general expenses. Again, at some of the Homes, such work as book binding and chicken raising has been successfully carried on. Independence is encouraged, and as soon as possible the girl is made to feel that, by aiding in the work of the Home, she can help meet the expense which she caused.

To the girl who has possibly never done sewing, never known anything about proper cooking or the care of a home, there is much that is new in this training, and, on the other hand, great patience is required on the part of her instructors. A fit of anger or despondency, and in a very short time she has left the Home and its care, and returned to her old life. Some do this even more than once and again return, having, upon reflection, realized the force of its love and shelter. Others, of course, leave and never return, but a large number are sent back to their own homes or out to fill situations of various kinds.

A great difference is found between one girl and another, due to the different status of life and surroundings from which they originally fell; hence, some girls are reformed with greater ease and in a shorter time than are others. The average time that a girl is retained in the Home is about four months. The Army aims at keeping in touch with them afterwards.

"Personally," says one of the leading Rescue officers writing on this point, "I attach by far the greatest importance to the work done with our girls after they leave the Home. If we ceased our care for them when they went out to service, we should have, I fear, many failures. I have by my elbow, as I write to you, a current record of 120 girls, not picked out but taken just as they come, which tells just where each one is, what she is doing, what was her spiritual condition when last seen or heard from, what day visited, etc. That list is taken from a record kept of every girl who passes through our hands. On one page is her previous life story; on the other, her career after leaving the Home. It is the most important record we keep." [90]

Along with other departments of social service in the Army, this department has been considerably extended during the past few years. Figures are at hand for the United States only. In 1896 there were five Rescue Homes with a total accommodation for 100 girls, and there were, in the Rescue Work, 24 officers. In 1904 we found twenty-two homes, with a total accommodation for 500 girls, and there were 110 specialized officers engaged in the Rescue Work. During the eight years prior to 1907 15,000 girls were helped. [91] Speaking of the year 1903-4, Commander Booth-Tucker says: "More than 1,800 girls passed through the homes during the year, and of these 93% were satisfactory cases, being restored to lives of virtue, while some 500 babies were cared for." [92] During the past few years, also, some valuable properties have been acquired for the purposes of Rescue Homes. Among these are two Homes in Philadelphia worth $20,000.00; the Home in Manhattan, New York City, valued at $35,000.00; the Home in Buffalo, costing nearly $40,000.00; the Home in Los Angeles, worth more than $15,000.00, and others.

In conclusion it may be said that although this great social question presents almost overwhelming problems for solution, yet there is no agency that deals with the evil in a curative way so successfully, and on such a scale, as does the Rescue Department of the Army. One difficulty of the work is that, while so many departments of the Army work are self-supporting, this work cannot be made so. Another difficulty is the lack of those who are willing to sacrifice their lives to such noble effort. Mrs. Catherine Higgins, former Secretary for this department, in her report, said that she had a great need of 100 more workers, and that she could use many times that number in the furtherance of the work.

While it is rather the part of society to strike at the very causes of this social evil and root it out entirely, still, such successful combating with the evil itself, right on the battle-field of flagrant vice, should receive the hearty support of all.

FOOTNOTES:

[88] Mentioned in Josiah Strong's Social Progress, 1906, p. 243.

[89] In Great Britain in 1903, the proportion of re-admissions in the Rescue Homes was about one in seven. In that year, about one-sixth of the new cases were unsatisfactory. (The S. A. and the Public, p. 131.)

[90] "Social Service in the Salvation Army," p. 71.

[91] Pamphlet "S. A. in the U. S."

[92] Ibid., p. 26.

CHAPTER VI.

Some Minor Features of the Salvation Army Social Work.

There are a number of features of the Salvation Army Social Work, which for the sake of brevity we shall group together in one final chapter. These are, (1): Christmas dinners, (2): prison work, (3): the employment bureau, and (4): work among the children. Taking up the subject of Christmas dinners, we find here what seems to be an advertising scheme more than a systematic form of relief. Sentiment, doubtless, has its place, even with the masses, and yet, in this great winter feast, there is more sentiment than there is real practical good accomplished. To the quiet, calculating student the question arises whether it would not be far better to utilize the vast amount of energy and financial outlay, which it gives to gorging the multitude for one day, in a better and more lasting way; the question whether there is not, in these Christmas feasts, a likeness to the old time feast of pagan Rome. In every city of any size throughout the country the pots and kettles on the street corner are familiar objects. At each Corps or other location of the Army, tickets are given out entitling the bearer to a Christmas dinner, or, in certain cases, to a basket with a dinner for a family. A good deal of trickery is indulged in by the professional beggars, by means of which it often happens that several dinners go to the same person. And yet, as we have watched those 5,000 baskets containing food for 25,000 persons go out, to bring cheer and comfort to the hungry in their homes, and as we have gazed on that vast banquet of 3,000 guests seated at one sitting, we could not but feel glad that these poor brothers and sisters of ours might realize the force of human sympathy for once in the year at least. [93]

Another minor feature of the Salvation Army work is the prison work. The majority of the jails, local, county and state, are visited at intervals by certain members of the Army set aside for that purpose in each community. In one State's prison there is a regularly organized corps of Salvation Army soldiers, who are all prisoners, some of them for a life term. In most prisons the Army provides literature, sees to the correspondence of the prisoners and holds meetings with them. But it is not so much the work with the prisoners in the jail that counts, as it is the influence gained over them, which leads them to come to the Army and make a new start in life when they get out. Many who find themselves behind the prison bars are not to be classed as regular criminals. A man is often classed as a criminal who is a victim of misfortune only, and has no inherent criminal instincts. It is with the criminal "by occasion," as Lombroso puts it, [94] that much successful work can be done in the way of reform. The Army has a regular organization known as the Prison Gate League. When a prisoner is discharged he is met by one of this league and invited to go to work at one of the Army's institutions. After being influenced and helped in this institution for a certain length of time, if he seems to justify it, he is sent out to work in some position. There are no definite statistics recorded of those of this class who have been permanently bettered.

Still another minor feature is the employment bureau system. While mentioned here as merely one of a group of minor features, this system is one of great importance to the industrial world. It is being taken into consideration in many places by thoughtful men, and there is promise of its assuming national, if not international proportions. The general term, employment bureau, serves to bring to our recollection the accompanying evils of the contract wage system and industrial slavery, against which there has been agitation in the past, but it is because of these accompaniments that the importance arises of securing a system which shall be free from them. In Germany considerable work has been done along these lines, municipalities and provinces have taken up the work, and an all-round effort is being made to place labor in the right position for work at the proper time. [95] New York City is to-day swarming with many agencies, which are conducted by men and women, who may rightly be classed as extortioners. In spite of the rigid rules on the subject, the ignorance and poverty of their victims makes evasion of the law comparatively easy. Jacob A. Riis, speaking of this subject, says:

"It is estimated that New York spends in public and private charity every year around eight millions. A small part of this sum intelligently invested in a great labor bureau that would bring the seeker of work and the man with work together, under auspices offering some degree of mutual security, would certainly repay the amount of the investment in the saving of much capital now much worse than wasted, and would be prolific of the best results." [96]

In regard to the work of the Army in this field every large city contains an employment bureau conducted by it and maintained for the free use of the unemployed. Some of the men, who secure positions have been in one of its own institutions, and the Army workers know whether or not to recommend them for a certain position. Outside of giving men work in its own institutions, the Army, during the year 1907, found employment for 55,621 persons in the United States alone.

Contrary to expectation, the children's work of the Army has not attained a magnitude in proportion to the other lines of work which have been developed. This may be accounted for in part by the fact that there are more institutions open for children to which the Army can turn for help than there are institutions of other types. Thus, while the Army can often get a child taken into some orphanage already existing, either public or private, in the case of the drunkard, the unemployed or the fallen woman, the Army finds it necessary to furnish its own institutions. Again, the Army states that wherever possible, some friend is found who is willing to adopt a child. Of course, this is far preferable to placing the child in some institution, inasmuch as adoption restores the home in a real sense.

The work among the children may be divided into temporary work and permanent work. By temporary work we do not mean work that is superficial, for it may be the most permanent and lasting in its results, but we mean work that is undertaken which influences the children for a limited amount of time only. The slum nursery or kindergarten is of this type, but as we have already described it in connection with the Slum Department, it needs only mention here. Another line of temporary work is the Sunday School work of the Army, but that comes under the religious work and not the social.

An important line of temporary work, however, is the summer outing for the poor children. In each of our large cities these excursions for the poor children have been carried out on a large scale. Arrangements are made with a railroad or a steamboat company; the children are collected, hundreds at a time, and cared for by parties of Salvationists, they are taken out to the country for the day. Children who have never seen the country, and who do not know what a tree, a green hill, or the running water looks like, are thus given an entirely new outlook upon the world, and a lasting impression is made on their minds. In Kansas City, this line of work has been developed still further. One of the large parks has been handed over to the Army by the city authorities, and in it has been established a summer camp. Tents are pitched on the grass under the trees, and poor families are brought out here for a week at a time. In this way hundreds of families have experienced a little of summer vacation who otherwise would never have left their slum dwellings.

The permanent handling of the children as opposed to the temporary, begins with the Maternity Homes which are managed in connection with the Rescue Homes, and continues on through the Orphanages. The children cared for in this permanent way are the babies from the Maternity Homes and orphans. From this it must not be supposed, with regard to the Maternity Homes, that there is any intentional separation or even a suggested separation of the child from the mother, but in many cases, after a time, a partial separation is necessary. The mother is influenced and taught to care for and love her offspring, but after spending some months in the Home, she may take a situation of some sort, often as a domestic servant, and here she cannot take her baby. Hence, in such cases, the mother is expected to visit her child frequently, and to provide for its support.

The other class of children dealt with in a permanent way are those who are picked up from the street, or who otherwise fall into the hands of the Army, often after being deserted by their parents. While Orphanages, as already stated, are not an important item in the Army's work, there are several in England and four in the United States. For the situation of an Orphanage, a country location is sought. For instance, one near New York City is located on a beautiful piece of property at Spring Valley. Another is at Rutherford, N. J. One of the largest is situated near San Francisco, California, and one of the latest additions for this purpose has been the securing of a fine piece of property at Lytton Springs, Cal. In all, there is accommodation for two hundred and twenty-five children in the United States.

FOOTNOTES:

[93] The author refers here to the annual Christmas dinner given in New York.

[94] "The Criminal," p. 208.

[95] "The German Workman," ch. XVII

[96] "How the Other Half Lives," p. 253.

CHAPTER VII.

Conclusion.

We have now covered the work of the Salvation Army social movement in its different branches. We have described the work, the extent and the management of each department. We have also considered the criticisms and objections to which each department is open, and we have attempted to estimate the value of each department to society. We have arrived at the conclusion that the work of the Industrial Department, leaving out the Industrial Colony, is a practical, deserving and successful effort to put unfortunate men once more on their feet, at no expense to the public, saving a slight embarrassment to those already engaged in the salvage and second hand business; that the Army lodging house is the best so far offered for the housing of the lower homeless class, although not entirely satisfactory; that the Slum Work is good, but limited in its scope, owing to the religious sentiment attached, and the mental inferiority of its workers; that the Rescue Work is about the best of its kind; and that good work is being done in other directions, such as the prison work, the employment bureaux and the children's work. On the other hand, we have found that the two Industrial Colonies and three Farm Colonies are not successful enough to warrant any additional expenditure on them or on any new colonies. This is due to the fact that the class most needing help in the cities is not the class to succeed on the land, and to the fact that men are more successful as pioneers on the land, when they are scattered and left to rely on themselves, having experienced farmers as neighbors, than when they are grouped closely together in one colony. Also there is nothing in favor of heavy expenditure for Christmas dinners, since the same amount of money can be put to better advantage in other ways.

But, having reached these conclusions regarding the separate departments of the Army social work, what about the movement as a whole? The critics have advanced a good many objections against the Army. Some of these objections relating to special departments and not to the Army as a whole, we have already dealt with in our discussion of those separate departments. There remain six principal objections:

1. That the organization is narrow and not willing to cooperate with other organizations.

2. That the highly centralized military form of government is likely to lead to disastrous consequences.

3. That the Army, in its financial dealings, does not take the public sufficiently into its confidence.

4. That the Army collects funds, on the strength of its social work, and applies these funds to religious propaganda.

5. That there is a lack of accuracy in its reports of work accomplished.

6. That the Army, as an organization, has become more of an end in itself, than a means to an end.

Regarding the first objection, the narrowness and lack of cooperation, we think there is a good deal of truth in it. The Army has made a great success as an organization, and the work of its founder and his assistants is one of the most remarkable achievements of the age. Things apparently impossible have been accomplished, and obstacles apparently unsurmountable have been overcome. The result is a self-confidence and assurance, amounting in many cases to bigotry. The members of the organization look upon it as especially favored by God, and as above any other organization. Hence, we find many of the leaders far from humble in their bearings, whatever their profession may be, and entirely uninclined to cooperate with other organizations. This fact has been brought to the foreground of late years in England and America by a certain amount of antagonism between the Army and the Charity Organization Society, the Army claiming that it can do its work along its own lines and get along without any alliance with the Society, and the latter claiming that much economy would result if the Army would unite its efforts along social lines with the Charity Organization Society. The controversy cannot be discussed here, but it seems a pity that some sort of union cannot be entered into in which both organizations would be represented in a manner satisfactory to both. One great difficulty, evidently, is the religious element in the social work of the Army, which tends to prejudice the Charity Organization Society in some degree against the Army, and tends to keep the Army aloof from any organization considered secular. However, we find many leading officers in both organizations with friendly feeling, and there is hope that the time will come, when the controversy will be at an end.

Coming to the second objection, that the highly centralized military form of government of the Army is likely to lead to disastrous consequences, we think that, if continued, this form of government must indeed lead to disaster. It is evident that this might happen in different ways. In an organization held together by one man or by one idea, disintegration would tend to take place in the one case by the failure or death of the leader, and in the other case by the expansion of the idea. The Army is held together by both the man and the idea, and we need not turn away from its own history to get examples of this disintegration in both ways. Take the first bond of union, the man of striking, hypnotic personality. Since the very inception of the movement, time after time, men who have gained influence in the Army, have separated from its ranks and started a movement of their own of more or less formidable dimensions. The instance most applicable here is that of the division which took place a few years ago in the United States. At that time the Army in this country had been very successful under the leadership of one of General Booth's sons, Ballington Booth and his wife, Maud, the latter especially being a most attractive and talented personality and gifted, persuasive speaker. Mr. and Mrs. Ballington Booth were flattered by attention from all sides, and by the worship of the soldiers and officers under them. Orders came from General William Booth, commanding them to give up their leadership in the United States and take control of some other country. But they had no idea of giving up their position in this country, and, elated by success, confidently announced their leadership of a new movement, the Volunteers of America, which is still in existence. While the other element, that of the expansion of the idea, showed itself at this time in a revolt against the narrow, despotic methods of General William Booth, the main element in this division was that of personality. Taking up the second bond of union, that of the central, controlling idea and purpose, we find the whole movement at the present time is tending to disintegrate through the expansion of this idea. This is shown by the continual departure of men from the ranks of the Army, who see that its methods and machinery are too cramped for their efforts, and also by the different attitude of the remaining members towards the movement itself and its leader General William Booth.

It is possible, however, that there will gradually be effected a change in the form of government of the army which will allow for enlargement and differentiation within the movement itself. General Booth, the sole head of the movement, cannot live much longer, and at his death, changes already threatening will demand attention. He has maintained a remarkable control over his world-wide following, in spite of numerous outbreaks and dangerous splits, and has legally arranged with great care, we are told, the succession to follow him. But that there will ever be a second General Booth, or that there could be a series of General Booths, able to hold the organization as he has, is incredible. We have talked with leading officers of his Army on this subject and find that they too, are looking for changes. The fact that the social work is having such a remarkable growth, while the spiritual work is apparently unable to hold its own, is in itself a feature demanding a change. The Army of industrial and social officers and employees will not be bound by the same ties to the General as his former Army of spiritual officers and soldiers. The latter were possessed with an emotional, fanatical enthusiasm which blinded them to everything save the service of their much adored General. The former have a different outlook on life. They are the new Army, a result of tendencies inherent in the growth of the movement. They look at humanity and individuals from other standpoints than that of the salvation of the soul. The material side of society, with its institutions of business, and practical forms of charitable relief, occupies a large amount of their attention. This has already led to considerable differentiation of government and control. Take, for example, the corporation, "The Industrial Homes Company" controlling eighty-four industrial institutions in the United States, and managed by a board of directors in New York City. This example is opening the way toward a future government by a board of some sort for other departments of the Army, and in time for the spiritual department, and then the further step of representation of members on these boards will not be far distant. At any rate we see reason for hoping that, while other improvements are taking place, the government of the Army will not be a handicap to the movement.

By the third objection, that the Army in its financial dealings does not take the public sufficiently into its confidence, is meant that complete records of detailed expenditure are not issued. The public provides for a large part of the income of the Army, and it has a right to know just how and where that income is spent. The man and woman who is being continually confronted by a lassie on the street with a little box for the receipt of contributions, after contributing again and again, is likely to ask the question, just where is this money going; and it would be of advantage to the Army itself, if it would issue a more definite statement of the use to which it puts public money. Some people are satisfied with the general report that "the

Army is doing good," but there are many who would contribute more largely, if they knew directly for what they were contributing. In reply to this criticism, the Army states that it deposits regularly with the state authorities a statement showing the disposition and state of the finances of its corporations, such as "The Reliance Trading Company" and "The Salvation Army Industrial Homes Company."

The Army also issues every year a balance sheet which shows its assets and liabilities on a large scale. But this is not sufficient. The ordinary person can receive no light from either the statement deposited with the state authorities or the yearly balance sheet published by the Army. In fact, although the Army uses the services of an expert accountant in getting out this balance sheet, for all that the public knows, it may be using the funds entrusted to it in any way it wishes. This should be remedied by a regular statement, clearly revealing the disposition of every cent donated.

A discussion of the preceding objection leads us to the fourth objection, that the Army collects funds on the strength of its social work, and applies these funds to the carrying on of its religious propaganda. [97] The Army denies this, but admits that there is a good deal of money collected for the general work, there being no specific object implied when it is collected, other than a statement of the various departments in which the Army is working, and of their extent. Of course, the social work comes in for strong presentation on the statement, but the money not being collected for any one object, the Army is at liberty to apply it to any branch of its work whether spiritual or social. This again shows the need of greater definiteness and accuracy in the Army's report to the public.

A fifth objection is the lack of accuracy shown by the Army in its reports of work accomplished. [98] This has special reference to the statistics published by the Army, and is a good criticism. At different times and in different parts of the world, statistics are given out, which seems to emanate from no one authority, which are often contradictory, and which create confusion in the mind of the person wishing to get at the facts. As a result of a good deal of recent criticism on this point, all future statistics of the Army in the United States are to come from one point only, are to be in charge of an expert, and no publication of statistics is to be allowed without the consent of the National Headquarters.

The sixth and last objection is a very important one and one which has been seen in the history of organizations without number, viz: that the organization tends to become an end in itself, instead of a means to an end. This objection is also allied to a former one regarding a lack of cooperation on the part of the Army with other organizations. More and more an organization, formed as is the Army, feels complete in itself, and works continually for its own interests and its own glory. In a large number of instances the objective point that was once humanity and the glory of God tends to become the advancement of the Army. While feeling that this objection is a serious one, it still cannot be considered as anything but unavoidable, considering the government and general character of the movement. If it were possible for the Army to be governed locally, and to some extent, nationally by boards, a part of whose membership represented the public, we believe that the tendency to advance its own interest would be diminished. Study out the workings and control of this organization, and it is found a machine, ever seeking to increase its power and field of work. If this machine could be controlled to some extent by the public which feeds it, it might be kept as a useful servant, but otherwise, in spite of the great service which it does society to-day, the tendency to get away from its object and to become an object itself, will be more and more dangerous.

In conclusion, then, we find that these objections advanced by the critics are not without foundation, and while some may be more tendencies than actualities, it lies with the organization to guard itself from them. We have found the Army an efficient worker along several lines, and society owes it a considerable debt for past service and lessons learned from it. Hence it would be a great pity for its efficiency as a great public servant to be lessened by a lack of publicity regarding its finance, or by a narrow, self-centered policy, or by a too centralized form of government. Some of the Army leaders are men of great hearts and strong minds, and it is to be hoped that, whenever in the future, the opportunity offers to make a beneficial change of policy in its duty toward the public or toward its sister organizations engaged in charitable work or in its own internal administration, that these leaders will stand firmly for what they believe, and demand the necessary change.

FOOTNOTES:

[97] See the "S. A. and the Public," Ch. 5.

[98] See the "Social Relief Work of the S. A.," p. 4.

BIBLIOGRAPHY.

American Journal of Sociology, Volume III.

Besant, Sir Walter,

The Farm and the City,

Contemporary Review, 72-792.

Booth, Bramwell,

I. A Day with the Salvation Army,

S. A. Press, London, 1904.

II. Illustrated Interviews,

S. A. Press, London, 1905.

Booth, Charles,

Life and Labor of the People,

The Macmillan Co., New York, 1899.

Booth, Commander Eva,

Where Shadows Lengthen,

S. A. Press, New York, 1906.

Booth, Florence E.

A Peep into My Letter Bag,

S. A. Press, London, 1905.

Booth, William,

I. In Darkest England, and the Way Out,

S. A. Press, London, 1890.

II. Social Service in the Salvation Army,

S. A. Press, London, 1903.

III. The Doctrines of the Salvation Army,

S. A. Press, London.

IV. The Why and Wherefore of the Rules and Regulations of the Salvation Army,

S. A. Press, London.

V. Orders and Regulations for Field Officers,

S. A. Press, London.

Booth-Tucker, Commander,

I. William Booth, Life of

S. A. Press, New York, 1898.

II. The Salvation Army in the United States,

S. A. Press, New York, 1899.

III. Social Relief Work of the Salvation Army in the United States,

S. A. Press, New York, 1900.

IV. Our Future Pauper Policy in America,

S. A. Press, New York, 1898.

V. Prairie Homes for City Poor,

S. A. Press, New York, 1899.

VI. A Review of the Salvation Army Land Colony in California,

S. A. Press, New York, 1903.

Coates, Thomas F. G.

The Prophet of the Poor,

E. P. Dutton & Co., New York, 1906.

Dawson, William Harbutt,

The German Workman,

Chas. Scribner's Sons, New York, 1906.

Devine, Edward T.,

The Principles of Relief,

The Macmillan Co., New York, 1905.

Hadleigh,

The Salvation Army Colony,

S. A. Press, London, 1904.

Haggard, H. Rider,

The Poor and the Land,

Longmans, Green & Co., New York, 1905.

Higgins, Mrs. Catherine,

Love's Laborings in Sorrow's Soil,

S. A. Press, New York, 1904.

Huxley, T. H.,

Social Diseases and Worse Remedies,

The Macmillan Co., New York, 1891.

Manson, John,

The Salvation Army and the Public,

E. P. Dutton & Co., New York, 1906.

Precipices: A Sketch of Salvation Army Social Work,

S. A. Press, London, 1904.

Report of Committee of Fifteen,

The Social Evil,

G. P. Putnam's Sons, New York, 1902.

Report of the Departmental Committee, Appointed to Consider Mr. Rider Haggard's Report on Agricultural Settlements in British Colonies.

Wyman & Sons, London, 1906.

Riis, Jacob A.,

I. How the Other Half Lives,

Chas. Scribner's Sons, New York, 1902.

II. The Children of the Poor,

Chas. Scribner's Sons, New York, 1902.

III. A Ten Years' War,

Houghton, Mifflin & Co., New York, 1900.

IV. The Peril and Preservation of the Home,

Geo. W. Jacobs' & Co., Philadelphia, 1903.

Ruskin, John,

Sesame and Lillies,

Donohue, Hernneberry and Co., Chicago.

Seager, Henry Rogers,

Introduction to Economics,

Henry Holt and Co., New York, 1908.

Selected Papers on the Social Work of the Salvation Army,

S. A. Press, London, 1907.

Solenberger, Edwin D.,

The Social Relief Work of the Salvation Army,

Byron & Willard Co., Minneapolis, 1906.

Swan, Annie S.,

The Outsiders,

S. A. Press, London, 1905.

Warner, Amos G.,

American Charities,

T. J. Crowell & Co., New York, 1894.

VITA.

The author of this dissertation, Edwin Gifford Lamb, was born in London, England, December 22, 1878. He attended private schools in that city and then spent three years in Northwestern Canada without schooling. After this he went to California where he prepared for college in the preparatory department of the University of the Pacific. He became a citizen of the United States as soon as eligible and graduated from Leland Stanford Junior University in 1904, with the degree of A. B. In the year 1904-'05, he was a student at Union Theological Seminary and Columbia University. During the year 1905-'06, he held a scholarship in Sociology at Columbia University. At this institution he studied under Professors F. H. Giddings, John B. Clark, H. R. Seager, H. L. Moore, J. Dewey, F. J. E. Woodbridge and W. P. Montague. Since that time he has been an instructor in the Harström School, Norwalk, Connecticut.

Made in United States
Orlando, FL
01 December 2023